D1356357

THE FIRST NATION
IN EUROPE

A PORTRAIT OF SCOTLAND
AND THE SCOTS

DAVID MURRAY

PALL MALL PRESS,
LONDON

Copyright: David Murray 1960

First published: 1960

Published by The Pall Mall Press Limited,
2 Clement's Inn, Strand, London, W.C.2,
and printed by Charles Birchall & Sons Ltd.
Liverpool and London.

To my Mother

Ann MacFarlane

better known in Ard Tong in the Lewis
as Anna, *nighean Alasdair mhic Pharlan.*

"A mother's breath is aye sweet. . .
. . . is *blath anail na mathar. . .*"

. . . . and to

John Knox,

Andrew Melville and George Buchanan

" For the transgression of a land,
many are the princes thereof; but by a
man of understanding and knowledge,
the state thereof shall be prolonged."

CONTENTS

CHAPTER ONE

FIRST NATION IN EUROPE

IN the spring of the year 1603, James Stewart, King of the Scots, and the sixth of his name, hurriedly took the road to London as the acclaimed heir to the crown of Elizabeth the First, lately Queen of England and mistress of Ireland. His claim, vouched for by the Lord Mayor and the Aldermen, with five hundred citizens, all well mounted and with chains of gold about their necks, rested on the fact that she and his grandfather were first cousins. That relationship had come about by virtue of the marriage of Margaret Tudor, daughter of Henry the Seventh of England, to James the Fourth, King of the Scots.

The now long dead Henry had looked far forward to such an event. Pressed to say what might happen if, out of his marriage-making, a Scot came to sit on the throne of England, he affirmed that 'the greater would draw the less'. Out of a series of bloody passages, the time for that process to begin now seemed at hand.

James the Fourth, who wore an iron belt as a constant reminder of his father, who had been murdered after being routed by his own nobles at Sauchieburn, fell at Flodden by the arms of his brother-in-law, Henry the Eighth of England. His son, James the Fifth, died of a broken heart on hearing of the sorry defeat of his men at Solway Moss, by the forces of his own uncle. As he turned to the wall on his deathbed, he muttered of the Royal Stewart line: 'It cam wi' a lass, and it'll gang wi' a lass.' His own lass, Mary, Queen of Scots, was put to death on the block by command of her second cousin, Elizabeth, Queen of England. Since Mary's son became James the First of England, King of Great Britain, France and Ireland, Scotland has had no resident monarch. Since the Estates of Scotland adjourned in January, 1707, after merging their affairs with the Parliament of England, the country has had no domiciled legislature.

9

Yet in all the years since Queen Mary and her consort King William sat on their joint throne, the dream of Henry the Seventh has never come to pass. For all the overt and covert pressures to conform to the model of England, the spirit of nationhood still beats strong in Scotland and is now waxing ever stronger.

Why that should be, and what it portends are the concerns of this book. It is not taken up with the fleeting and mostly turbulent procession of monarchs and great people. It seeks to show the significance, alike to England as to Scotland, of such straws in the wind as the meeting of the most of the Members of Parliament returned by Scotland (a good few of them strangers to the country) in Glasgow in the spring of 1960. There had never been such a convention in Scotland in over 250 years.

To set the scene, a nation may be defined as a community of people, commanding all the means for a viable independent life, in a clearly demarcated country, and cleaving to its own distinctive ways.

On these scores, the Scots are undoubtedly a nation. They were moreover the first people in all Europe to set themselves apart as a nation. The essential borders of their land have not changed in any degree for a thousand years. What time the frontiers of other nations, including that which came to be the English nation, have moved this way or that, have extended or completely vanished, Scotland has remained bounded by the sea and the line of the Cheviots. The Border town of Berwick at the mouth of the Tweed, which was reft out of the Scottish kingdom by force of arms almost five hundred years ago, has remained Scottish in every respect that matters. For all its mayor and aldermen, it has the look and feeling of a Scottish town. If occupied Berwick has resisted of itself the changes pressed upon it by England, how much more has the whole kingdom of Scotland?

To understand how a range of low green hills has remained so long the land bastion of a separate and distinct nation, with all its abiding attributes, one need only cast up the general and particular parts of the country. These should be viewed, not only as they are to-day, but also as they were five hundred, one thousand and two thousand years ago. A stretch of firm green sward may have been an impassable morass in the not so distant past. The sea which is now a highway was once a forbidding watery barrier.

The Scots, of whatever race or origin have been protected and moulded by the land in which they live. Their customs and habits, religions and laws, tongues and modes, social and political attitudes, their schooling, music, songs, dances, sports, and all their institutions match the natural land.

Their nationhood is an outcome of the interplay of those same ecological forces that set apart, modify after their kind, and hold in balance the creatures and growths of the wild. Their sense of national unity derives from a balanced diversity. In Scotland no one region could ever dominate another. Though it was often aspired, no class of people could ever put its foot or its sword to the neck of another, and hold it. The country itself always brought succour. As it sharpened the weapons of the commonalty, it blunted those of such people as in every country under the sun aspire to dominion and spare no pains to achieve it, though it may mean bartering their native land to strangers.

In Scotland, the Borderer, the Lowlander, the Highlandman and the Isleman all live and work to essentially different patterns. They talk English, or braid Scots, or the ancient Gaelic tongue. On the face of things, the industrial worker in the crowded towns has apparently little in common with the crofter along the sparsely settled western seaboard or on the scattered islands. The pale faced austere academician may seem far apart from the ruddy, throaty farmer of Lanarkshire, far less of the Mearns and Aberdeenshire. The business tycoon may match the shipyard labourer and the collier very ill. But both at home and against the world they are all unmistakably 'brither Scots'.

They warm to a feeling of abiding brotherhood that cannot be encompassed in the larger realm of England. They are not anything like so exercised with that concept of class which bedevils the English. They are not so defensive as the Welsh, nor so troubled about ancient wrongs and spoiling for a fight as the Irish. On occasion, of course, they have to raise their voices loud. But that's to counter the din from ten times their number in the south.

This Scottishness may seem very odd to the outsider, considering that, at first glance on a flat map, Scotland appears as merely the northern appendage of that conjointed island which has come to be known as Great Britain, compared with the lesser Brittany across the channel. But, though tied by land, the two near neighbouring countries of Scotland and England are markedly different in every natural respect. They have thus inexorably conditioned the generality who live in them to different philosophies and manners of life. Though the change may await the new generation the Englishman transplanted in Scotland becomes, in time, a Scot. Some of the most ardent 'Home Rulers' are in fact wholly or partly of English blood. The Scot who, for choice, sets up his permanent abode in England is well on the way to becoming an Englishman. Many who have not yet divested themselves of the 'Mac' (meaning 'son of') in their surnames have come to be more English than the true born Saxons themselves.

Taking each at large, the two countries are really no more alike than the northern and southern halves of Loch Lomond. That single body of fresh water, so much of a unity in Scottish song and story, divides into two quite distinct regions. The upper part is long, narrow, deep and mountain girt, like a typical Highland loch. The lower end is broad and shallow, with a studding of islands and low rolling shores. It is like a tame lake, in a softer clime. The two conjoined sheets of water each support their own marine and riparian life, after their quality. The difference of a few miles is a profound ecological factor. The mysterious 'powan', miscalled a 'freshwater herring', spawns in the cold water trapped in the Highland part and feeds at the lower end which catches the sun. It has survived by that juncture of advantage.

For a start, Scotland is far more exposed to the cold and stormy Atlantic than England. It is also more hilly and mountainous and much more sharply divided into regions. At the same time, the coast line is deeply indented, especially on the west, and is skirted by chains of islands.

Just above the Borders, where the general scene changes abruptly, the uplands of what are called, with some licence, the Lowlands, form a natural if somewhat diverse division. Galloway, in the south west corner is a land apart, a sort of detached Highlands.

The edging of coast on either side of the Lowlands, the narrow waist between the Forth and Clyde estuaries, the belt of farm land running up the east shore and round by the Moray Firth form another department.

Ramparted by the Grampians, and well away from the east coast, the mountain land, with its glens and straths, makes up the

Highlands. That distinct region is cut right through by the Great Glen, with its string of lochs.

The deeply serrated western seaboard, north of the Firth of Clyde, is again different. So also are the islands that lie out in the Atlantic, in the double chain of the Inner and Outer Hebrides. These islands, it may be said, are all quite different in aspect, with different founts of life.

Various other odd bits and pieces might be cited. For example, Caithness in the far north-east beyond the mountains of Sutherland has little in common with the Highlands proper. To the people of that wedge of flat land the mountains shrouded the country of the Southrons, hence Sutherland—so far north.

Away out in the cold ocean to the north, the Orkney and Shetlands islands are again not only quite different from the Hebrides, but also widely varied among themselves, as groups and individually. Especially in the Shetlands, the land and sea economy still retains remnants of the systems practised by the Norse before their rule was supplanted by the Scots. Needless to say, the people of those parts, the only Scottish colonists still tied politically to the Motherland, rather fancy themselves as hardy Vikings, though their blood, hair and tongue belie that role. Ulster, planted largely by Lowlanders, and Nova Scotia and Cape Breton in Canada, settled mainly by Gaelic-speaking Highlanders, are in some ways even more Scottish, though long since plying their own politics.

All these regions have nurtured different growths. These include, if not so very different looking human beings (though the round heads have congregated in the east, and the long heads in the west) then different attitudes of mind and ways of life. Touching on this natural segregation, it is one of the common saws when English people keep on referring to England when they mean Britain, as of the navy, or Britain when they really signify England, as about education, to hint that while all the obtuse Angles remained in the south, the acute Angles came north.

All the geographic and topographic attributes of the country must be assessed in terms of their conditioning effect years ago, and not only now.

For example, the sea, with the warm Gulf Stream flowing not far off the west coast to lose itself in the northern deep, is the main architect of the Scottish climate. It tempers the extremes of heat and cold and moistens the air. Thus, Glasgow, and distant

Stornoway, are warmer than London in the winter, but chillier and wetter in the summer. Together with the valley between the Clyde and the Forth, the sea produces that clammy cold 'haar' which seasonally makes fire loving students of the people of Edinburgh. The cold air over the North Sea rolls back the soft westerlies which funnel over from the Atlantic. Largely because of these golf course emptying visitations and the need to probe their mystery, Edinburgh has kept daily weather records since 1731 (with a brief break in between) that is to say, longer than any place on the face of the earth.

The sea very manifestly has profoundly influenced all the vegetable and animal growths of Scotland and in Scottish waters. It has given the country a good half of the British herring fishing, and, by its effect on the wind, it has presented it with a virtual monopoly of seed potato culture and traffic.

Perhaps less evidently, it has been a powerful factor in keeping the Scots as 'a' Jock Tamson's bairns' while the near neighbouring English have arrived at a very rigid social stratification. That has come about by the protection afforded by the sea in distant times before it became an easily navigable highway. It was the cold sea that left Scotland free to embattle a short land frontier against invaders in overwhelming force.

In the far off days when the deep sea was a source of terror, the land that is now England was subjected to heavy seaborne assaults and to successive conquests across a narrow channel by the Romans, Angles, Danes and Normans. But for their part, the various regions in Scotland were left free to work out their own individual, and ultimately their common destiny. Even when the wild Norsemen took to setting out to the open sea in fair force in their long boats, they managed to land only comparatively small detachments. They never succeeded in settling any numerous community, as the Danes did at York in England. To be sure, the Scots, who at length gave their name to the country, came by sea from Ireland, but by way of infiltration in small numbers into an empty mountain-walled coast land.

Bearing on the community wrought by the guarding sea and the mountains, a Scots lord likes to tell the story of the English nobleman who came to visit him, at his castle. Walking in the garden after port and cigars, the Scots lord blithely enquired of the old man with the barrow: 'Well, Bob, how are you getting on with the potting?' Taking his cue, the English gallant chipped in to the conversation in the same familiar terms. Drawing him aside, the Scots lord quietly counselled: 'You can't call Mr. MacCodrum Bob.' 'Why not?' rejoined the English lord, who meant well enough. 'You're calling him Bob.' 'Oh yes,' said the master of the house, 'but he's an old friend of mine, and you are still a stranger."

CHAPTER TWO

THE MIXING OF THE RACES

IT really matters little whence came, how spoke and who were the Brythonic, Goidelic, Celtic or Pictish tribes that drove the little dark firbolgs underground to peep out years later as bright-eyed, green-mantled fairies. What matters is that the peoples who settled the land known to the Romans as Caledonia, held and threw back the legions. The Romans were compelled to stand to arms behind Hadrian's stone wall between the Solway and the Tyne and, for a short spell, on the south side of Antonine's earthern rampart and ditch between the Clyde and the Forth. They were roughly handled when they ventured a few marauding expeditions farther north.

'Give me back my legion,' lamented the Roman Emperor as the Ninth vanished into the hills and never returned. Beyond their camps and defences the Romans, who overran almost all England and planted that country with villas and bath houses, left little imprint on Scotland. Nor did they pick up and record very much information about the long sworded warriors who, with the natural country to help them, set the armoured men with the short stabbing swords at defiance. Other than 'travellers' tales' of the painted Picts, very little is recorded in written history about the races who anciently held the land now known as Scotland. Some, so the chroniclers say, were Christians a full century before Constantine professed that faith in Rome. What is more certain is that more were evangelised by Saint Ninian from Galloway in the years following 400 A.D.

Christianity was spread still further by those Scots, from Ireland, whose name was eventually given to the land. From their visage, hair and tongue, it may have been, as some say, that these immigrants had come to a final halt after long ago wandering out of Scythia through Greece. With 'mille' for thousand, 'eaglais' for church, 'tir' for land, and many more, their tongue, which is still spoken in Scotland, certainly abounds in words that suggest a connection with the classical tongues of the Mediterranean. In the fifth century they began to settle along the sea lochs in the 'Land of the Gaels' which is now Englished as Argyll. There they set up their tiny kingdom of Dalriada. They called the mountain land to the west 'Alba', the name for Scotland that is still every day current among those who still speak the Gaelic language.

Along with their own well-developed native culture (they were choice workers in metal and enamel), these Scots brought a pastoral Christianity. Merging with the faith among the Picts, this supplanted the more authoritative Roman system well down into what is now England. The word was carried by the great evangel, St. Columba, who came from Ulster in the year 563 to labour from the islet of Iona. From this work, the saints who are well remembered in the north of present England, like Mungo in Cumberland, and Aidan and Cuthbert on the Holy Isle off Northumberland, were all Scots, as one might say.

The Columban missionaries gifted two main legacies. They warmed a feeling against prelates and their splendour, which tempered the Roman usage when it regained ground, and which has continued strong in Scotland to this very day. And by consolidating Dalriada and spreading their simple ideals among the neighbouring tribes, they paved the way for the union of the Picts and the Scots. They came together under Kenneth MacAlpine in the year 844. The united realm embraced the mainly mountain land between the two seas, and above the narrow neck pinched by the Forth and the Clyde. It was spined by the massifs of the Grampians. This country shortly became known as the land of the Scots, or Scotia.

By that time, the Britons, a race akin to the modern Welsh, occupied the valley of the Clyde and a coastal strip running far down the widening estuary of the river. The Anglian kingdom of Northumbria marched with the Forth. Various Pictish tribes still maintained their independence on either side of the bight of the Moray Firth in the north, and in Galloway, in the south west. The wild stranger Norse from the sea were in possession of the tip of Caithness and of much of the fringe of islands.

As the years passed, the now well defined Scots got on to terms of great friendship with the Britons of Strathclyde. They joined forces and at length, after varying fortunes in war, totally defeated the Northumbrians at Carham in the year 1018.

That victory brought the Merse or border country above the Tweed, and the Lothians, into the Scottish domain. It also, towards the height of the dominance of the Gaels, introduced that Saxon tongue which came to be the English language. That same year, the 'gentle Duncan' of Shakespeare's *Macbeth* succeeded by blood right to the throne of Strathclyde. In 1034, as grandson and heir of that Malcolm who had humbled the Anglian Northumbrians at Carham, Duncan also became King of the Scots. The style of that title signified that he was king by more than mere hereditary blood-right. His was a personal office, approved by the assembled people. He was thus monarch of most of the varied peoples on the mainland of what is now modern Scotland.

However, various independent jarls on the islands, mormaers in the north and chiefs in the west and south-west still went their own way. Duncan was killed by a strong man among them, the mormaer MacBeth. He was far from being the craven schemer that Shakespeare made out to his dramatic purpose. A man of valour and kingship he gave Scotland years of prosperity. But to Malcolm Canmore, the son of Duncan, so called for his *ceann mor* or big head, he was an usurper. Weakened by the Norse-stiffened Northumbrians who were set against him, he was at length defeated and slain at Lumphannan in Aberdeenshire on the 15th of August, 1057. That day, when MacBeth 'died with harness on his back' was the real birthday of the Scottish nation, that continued and exists to-day.

Since MacBeth was put to the sword in battle over nine hundred years ago, the Scots have remained indisputably, if not always undisputedly a nation. They have remained a nation much more definitely and discernibly than the English ever have been, or can hope to be. With the cohesion of the peoples of the land and the settling of the forms of rule, the raids of the Norsemen, who were not finally repelled until the battle near Largs in 1263, and the following incursions of the English, became incidental to their course. So also were their own excursions into England, beyond Durham to York, and the movement of the land frontier this way and that until it finally hardened where nature designed.

For all the internal tumults and external assaults, the Scots have maintained their essential boundaries unbreached (save only for the taking of the Scottish Royal Burgh of Berwick in 1482) and their common national spirit unimpaired for almost a thousand years. No nation in all Europe can match that enduring entity, neither growing out of all recognition, nor shattering into parts. From the time, long after the founding of the city, when the asylum by the Tiber came to be a power, until the irruption of the barbarians, great Rome lasted little longer.

It is not that the Scots always have been, nor are to-day a band of angelic brothers. Far from that, much of their story is written in blood spilled by fathers, brothers, sons and near kin, and betimes by mothers, sisters, and daughters. But the country itself has always healed those human frailties and nourished an abiding unity against the outer world, and, in special, against neighbouring England, both in peace and war. The robust nationhood of the Scots springs from the land itself. It is invigorated by the very air, and watered by the streams. Truth to tell, it would have made little difference if many of the painted Picts had been runaway Romans. Some, having regard to the amorous traffic at frontier posts, very probably were. Nor would it have mattered much if the Scots themselves had come straight from the Ionian isles, speaking Greek. As the scientists have now discovered, the seed of the troopers of Cromwell who were left unrecalled on the Aran islands is much nearer the Saxon blood than the generality in London. But these folk are now the most Irish of the Eirannachs.

Harking back, it should be remembered that the Romans came to Caledonia at the end of a long and tiring march. Loving their creature comfort, they were as much repelled by the winter snow and sleet, the all-the-year-round rain, the rough country and the poor prospect of winning any riches, as by long swords and spears. These natural hazards, on the other hand, would be no great deterrent to the immigrant Scots. That was all the more so since they came into an empty part of the country in small groups in frail craft, with no standards raised and no brazen trumpets blowing. Besides, as they multiplied and spread, they encountered people very much like themselves. Though there were armed struggles, the 'Scottish Conquest', as the historians term it, was on the whole a process of slow colonisation and integration.

While the incoming Scots were satisfied with the land as they found it, and content to remain, the Norse out of the creeks really sought bigger and better fish to fry, and more sunshine. While glad enough to make landfalls on the coast, they soon moved their main forces to where the climate and the booty were better, and the going less tough. At any rate, the Vikings never won a sizeable lodgment on the main territory of Scotland, as they did in England and Ireland and in those lands from Normandy to Sicily and far beyond where they followed the sun and sought the juice of the grape. Where they did manage to settle, as in Caithness and on the islands, they did not extirpate or expel the natives. Indeed, they were mostly content to take the local women to wife.

The place names and the language in the Hebrides bear present witness to that mixing. Four-fifths of the names of the townships are of Norse origin, from the husbandmen who first tamed the grudging soil. But the still prevailing mother's tongue is Gaelic, from the women who baked the cakes and bore the children. Some of the villages have a double-tongued name, like Ard Tong, where the Gaelic *ard* and the Norse *tong* mean the same point of land. That indicates a time when the two races lived and mixed peaceably side by side. Incidentally, the old place names in Lanarkshire, and all down through Ayrshire to Galloway, are almost all from the Gaelic fount, though the spoken tongue has long since departed. The Machar in Wigtownshire is the same as the *machair*, the rough land running down to the sea, in the Uists.

No more did the Normans, the Frenchified Norsemen who conquered and held down practically all England, and a large part of Ireland, ever win a footing in Scotland by force of arms. They forayed across the Border and backed sides, all right. But when they came to settle it was by tacit invitation. And, as the names prefixed to the 'Declaration of Arbroath' which was sent to the Pope in 1320, affirm, they soon gave up their stranger titling.

However, the Norman Conquest of England did impinge on Scotland in several powerful ways. The Princess Margaret, sister of the disinherited Edgar the Atheling, was among the fleeing Saxons who found succour in the country. In 1070, she married Malcolm Canmore, the same Scottish king who had slain MacBeth.

As queen, she waged unremitting war against everything Scottish, the Gaelic tongue, the native church, which had again become very Celtic, and the whole way of life. Naming four of her sons after Saxon kings, she did her level best to mould the mainly

Celtic kingdom to the broken Saxon model. Doubtless she washed the feet of beggarmen and obtained great spiritual comfort, but she was a very 'sore saint' for Scotland. The slow retreat of the Gaelic language and the advance of the English dates from her time.

When the Normans themselves entered the country in numbers, especially during the reign of her son, David the First, a half-Saxon given to English ways, they brought with them new styles in architecture, new legal institutions and the feudal system. But like the mailed knights themselves, the buildings, legalities and feudalism were soon adjusted to the country. That villeinage, the forced labour of serfs, which long persisted in England and has left its deep marks on that country to-day, never even got a proper footing. It withered in the plantling and died out before the rooting. Moreover, direct Norman influence never penetrated at all into the mountains and islands of the Celtic clans. There, a knight in the armoured panoply of war was always at the mercy, as he would be to-day, of an arrow or of a black knife finding the chinks.

While England was visited by a succession of overturning invasions, by the Romans, Jutes, Saxons, Angles, Danes and Normans, Scotland stood firm behind the barrier of distance, the sea and the mountains.

As the signatories at Arbroath set out to the Bishop and Pope of Rome : 'this nation, having come from Scythia the Greater, through the Tuscan Sea, and the Pillars of Hercules ... could never be brought in subjection by any people how barbarous soever ... This Kingdom hath been governed by an uninterrupted succession of one hundred and thirteen Kings, all of our own native and Royal stock, without the intervening of any stranger. . . .'

That early consolidation, the gift of nature, has had a great bearing in the course of events in Scotland these last thousand years, and on the changing state of affairs within the country to-day. When the sea became less of a barrier and the attacks from the south began in earnest, Scotland had already achieved a tight nationhood, which transcended all regional differences and which dissolved all stranger infusions.

The common nationhood remained proof, alike against assault from the outside, and cleavage from the inside. The differentiated parts of the country continued to ensure that no one area could dominate another. They also made certain that the monarch remained significantly King of the Scots, and subject to their laws, and not, as in the South, King of England, and paramount over the land and all that's in it.

CHAPTER THREE

THE MAKING OF THE NATION

WHEN the Normans seized and garrisoned almost all England, they found themselves in a land ribbed with few natural barriers, where all roads led to London. They were thus able to impose on that country that system of feudalism which depends on land and power being parcelled out by a monarch at the centre, and then handed down, step by step, until the whole business rests on the backs of the labouring masses at the bottom. They themselves capped, pressed down and stiffened the stratified class society which still marks that country to-day. Echoes of it are sounded in every quarter. For instance, the Brain Trusters who perform on the wireless and television are positively obsessed with questions about social status, class accents and the old school tie generally.

In Scotland, however, the Norman feudal system borrowed from England never became a hard and oppressive reality, save here and there, and never at all in the Highlands and Islands. Though its tinselly trappings still drape Scots Law, it was as foreign to the country as parliamentary government to black Ghana. As it flourished for long in England, serfdom never really took root in Scotland. The short answer was that the field labourer could always take to the hills behind him, with a pretty good hope of tripping up and knifing the oppressive lord.

'In ahint yon auld fail dyke,
  I wot there lies a new slain knight;
  And naebody kens that he lies there,
  But his hawk, and his hound, and his lady fair . . .'

From their fastnesses, the barons in turn could always bid defiance to the king. Archibald Douglas, Earl of Angus, gained the name of 'Bell-the-Cat' from his open willingness to hang a warning signal right round the neck of the pretentious monarch.

He was in the party that hog tied Cochrane, a court favourite, and as such made Earl of Mar, and hanged him over the bridge at Lauder before the very eyes of his master, James the Third. As for the burghs, they never at any time truckled to the kings, lords and prelates who signed their founding charters. Nor, when the country had settled to a form after the defeat of MacBeth could any one region ever gather and move enough force to impose its will on another. As all the classes were kept in balance, the country lent itself to a sort of natural federalism, much like that obtaining among the differently peopled and tongued Swiss cantons.

Quite late in the day, in 1598, James the Sixth sought to plant a company of adventurers from Fife in the Lewis, in hopes of drawing riches from the herring fisheries. The island clansmen promptly salted their heads in barrels, to the number of hundreds, and boldly sent them back to Leith. The king's men who had been given leave to carry out such 'slauchter, mutilations, fyre raising and uther inconvenientis' as might be necessary were glad enough in the end to put the stormy Minch between them and the 'wickit Hielandmen'. Yet these same Gaels, who would suffer no sort of immigrant *herrenvolk* in their own isles were always willing and able to come together under the banner of the Scots when a common danger threatened from outside. Whatever their bloody quarrels, and the history of Scotland is a tale of murderous turbulence, the country itself banded them together against the outer world.

That was seen long ago at the stricken Battle of the Standard near Northallerton in Yorkshire in 1138. At that time, the Norman kingdom was weakened by killing dissension between the partisans of Matilda and Stephen. To the cry of 'Albannach, Albannach ... Scots, Scots ...' the hill men of Galloway rushed and were spitted on the southern spears. The kilted men from the mountains and remote islands hewed in vain against the armour-clad chivalry. As the monkish chroniclers relate, the Scottish army embraced 'Normans, Germans and English, Cumbrian Britons, Northumbrians, men of Teviotdale and the Lothians, Picts and Scots'.

A century-and-a-half later, the by then strongly marshalled Anglo-Normans carried their arms, in turn, deep into Scotland. Peace and 'rowth of ale and breid' in the land had fallen over a cliff at Kinghorn in Fife with the 'righteous godly, wise and kind, mild and merciful' Alexander the Third. The invaders were resisted, alike by the Celts and the Saxons, and by most of the Normans who had come to be at home in Scotland. They all came together under William Wallace, the knight of Elderslie. From his name, he was of the Cumbrian kin to the Welsh. After a victory at Stirling Bridge, he went down to defeat at Falkirk. Unlawfully tried in the Great Hall at Westminster, on almost the exact spot where President de Gaulle recently sat in honour, he was put to a barbarous end by command of Edward the First.

Believing, as monarchs generally come to do, that the spirit of a nation is wrapped up in trappings, that *Mollens Scotorum*, or Hammer of the Scots, broke the Great Seal of Scotland in four and carried it off with the Scottish Records, the Black Rood and the *Lia Fail* or Stone of Destiny on which the Scottish kings had been crowned. William Wallace knew better. He knew that the soul of a nation is nourished in that 'freedom which is a noble thing and gives man to have liking'. He also knew that a nation must be able to sustain itself materially. With that feeling, during his brief period as Guardian of Scotland, he wrote to the Hansa merchants of Hamburg, telling them that the Scottish ports were open to the world. For the times, it was a remarkable missive.

The enduring struggle was then taken up by Robert Bruce, a baron of the true blood of the Normans. He hardly knew where his heart lay, until his country inexorably called him to muster the 'Inglis' of the Lowlands and the 'Scottis' of the Highlands and Islands. After many travails, during which, as the old tradition goes, he drew courage from the seven times repeated effort of a spider to spin a web across the rafters of a hovel, he finally put the host of Edward the Second of England to utter rout on the field of Bannockburn. That victory, won on Sunday, the 23rd of June, 1314, set the seal on continuing Scottish independence. It was affirmed to the then Anglophile Pope John in the Declaration of Arbroath of 1320.

Subscribed by the leaders of the Scottish nation, the Declaration ran : '. . . For so long as there shall but one hundred of us remain alive, we will never submit ourselves to the dominion of the English. For it is not glory, it is not riches, neither is it honour, but Liberty alone that we fight and contend for, which no honest man will lose but with his life . . .' (The translation from the original

Latin is taken from the version circulated in 1703, when the incorporating union with England was then under discussion.)

There were still many more alarums and excursions before the English acknowledged the Independence of Scotland in the Treaty of Northampton of 1328. In the meantime, that troubled nation had done its king to death and raised a new one, Edward the Third.

It may be said that the English agreed, on the side, to return the Stone of Destiny. But the Dean and Chapter of Westminster Abbey ignored a writ from the High Sheriff and held on to it. Save for a recent brief jaunt to Scotland, where it rested for months in two separate parts, in a mason's yard and in an engineering workshop, and in divers other places, it has remained in their hands ever since; except for the numerous small chips that were, as one might say, souvenired. These fragments are now multiplying in a truly miraculous manner, but who can deny them. They do say, as the legend grows, that the 'Stone' now encases the prophecy, 'it cam wi' a lass and will gang wi' a lass'. Not that it matters, for Scotland is full of stones which might be shaped like that under the Coronation Chair.

In spite of the Treaty, the English kept up their *sturm und drang* to the north over the centuries that followed. The Scots, not unnaturally retaliated and sought allies where they could. They leagued with France in what came to be known as the 'Auld Alliance'. From time to time, they backed one or other of the warring factions in England. The English, for their part, and as obtains to this day, were hardly ever without the help of an 'English party' in Scotland. Time and again armies marched over the now closely defined Border. Sometimes they were thrown back by main force of arms. Very often the Scots were scattered and their farms, churches and towns were burned. In 1513, the 'Floo'ers o' the Forest were a' wede awa' ' at Flodden. But by their own harrying, and the scorched earth tactics of the Scots, the English were always put at nought by the country itself.

During all this struggle, the alchemy of time and land was steadily at work on the Scottish nation. The Border which had been crossed so easily by the evangelising 'saints' from the north, had become a broad belt of 'debatable land' and a real dividing barrier. On either side of this, the two neighbouring nations had become more and more distinct. The once near English tongue which had spread from the Lothians over the Lowlands, and up the long broad fringe of the east coast, had become foreign to the English ear. While the root basis of it remained closer to the original Saxon than southern English, it had become laced with Gaelicisms and studded with many French words. From the traffic with France, the milk cow of the Lowlands to this day comes to *s'approche*. And from the Gaelic usage of the definite article, the byreman 'gets *the* cold the day'.

To be sure, mere language is not, after all, the vital mark of a nation. If that were so all the various English speaking countries would house one nation, and in a narrower sense England itself would be home to several. But a continued differentiation does indicate a moving apart. From a position which was already far apart in its foundation, Scotland moved away farther in the fields of husbandry and commerce, politics and governance, law and religion.

The early English historians have, of course quite a lot to say about Scottish barbarism. But for long after the Normans conquered England, the yield of the Scottish fields was not so very different from those in the balmier south. David the First an even 'sorer saint' than his mother, Queen Margaret, had in fact very notable 'green fingers'.

In those early days, too, the commerce of Scotland was at least as well established as that of England. The level of life and learning in Scotland was indeed quite comparable with that in the south. This is vouched for by the curious story about the birth of Robert the Second, otherwise known as King Bleary, and the first of the Stewart line. His mother, Marjory Bruce, daughter of Robert Bruce and wife to Walter, the High Steward (hence the family name) fell off her horse on a journey from Paisley to Renfrew. Though pronounced dead, the native mediciners had skill enough to deliver her son by Caesarian section, and that in 1316, over 650 years ago. None the less, it cannot be gainsaid that, as the years went on, the English realm prospered more materially. It had the advantage of a better climate and greater convenience to the narrow seas.

But the Scots, though they did not advance so much, in the rude times, in the makings of creature comfort (the constant wars with England wasted their substance) made an increasingly better share out of the realitites of political power. Down to the common hind, they maintained their personal and corporate rights and liberties much more successfully than the English. There were too many hidden valleys and hills of refuge in the Lowlands for the barons to set themselves up in castles of well tended indolence. In the Highlands, the chiefs, as fathers of their kin, necessarily partook of the life of their clansmen. They never became landed noblemen, in that sense of the term, until mainly English arms made them so.

The king could never overawe the whole realm from a strong fortress. Nor could any single town, like Edinburgh, dominate the whole country, as London came to do in England. In point of fact, the Scottish capital tarried at Falkirk, Stirling, Perth, and a number of places other than Edinburgh, long after the English seat of government had settled in one city. Leaguing together from their very beginning, the Scottish towns all maintained a sturdy independence. They sent armed burghers, and not mere levied vassals, to all the wars. With the ultimate authority of arms in their hands, and a broken country at their backs, the common people got a better share of what little was going. There was never any question, as in England, of any set of people making out that it had other than red blood in its veins, giving entitlement to the finest raiment and the choicest cuts.

There were power-seeking men enough in Scotland, always willing to kill the king himself, as they did James the First and James the Third—and themselves into the bargain. But there were also plenty of farmers in the Lowlands fit and able to stand against them. The towns were full of sturdy characters like that crooked smith, Hal o' the Wynd, who fought in a gladiatorial mell at Perth for a crown and his own hand. In the Highlands and on the Islands, a man might be a gentleman though owning himself no more than a few rags and a *sgian dubh* (black knife). The wide diffusion of schooling in Scotland, centuries before it was anything like the common lot in England, was a sure sign that liberty was in the air, and, with that freedom, human dignity.

The scene was set by that chief among the MacLeans who, for curiosity's sake, was invited to dine at an English manor house. Being given a place well down the board, his man demurred. 'Oh well now,' said MacLean, 'dinna fash yoursel', Donald, where MacLean sits, that's the head of the table.' George the Third got a taste of this when, at his express request, two Highland private soldiers gave a display of the broadsword and the Lochaber axe in the gallery of his palace of St. James's. He gave them each a golden guinea. They dropped the coins into the hands of the porter at the gate.

All this proceeded from the nature and the balanced parts of the country. Contrive as he might, the king remained subject to the laws of the paramount people. That was indeed why 'Jamie the Saxt' was so ready to take himself and his notions about 'divine right' to England.

It was the same with religion. The Scottish nation never was prelatic, and never can be. In a land which did not favour showy pomp and ceremony, the most highly placed churchman had to remain close to the people, or give way. In its greatest days, the Roman Catholic church in Scotland was very native. Outside the realm, it owned no other authority than the Pope of Rome himself, as remains to-day. Nor were any princes of that church plainly murdered, like Thomas Becket in England, or humiliated, like Cardinal Wolsey. The last cardinal, David Beaton, was hung over the battlements at St. Andrews, *for his cruelty*. The last ruling archbishop, John Hamilton, was hanged in his canonicals *for his rebellion*, being found in arms against the nation at Dumbarton Castle.

The argument is that, until the time of MacBeth and Malcolm Canmore, Scotland, ringed by the sea and buttressed by the hills, was free to develop a strong national constitution that was sound enough to withstand the testing times which followed. Conjointly with the country, these same years of trial put even more bone and sinew into the body of the nation. It has thus stood firm over the later centuries of 'incorporating union' with England.

CHAPTER FOUR

SCOTS LAW

WHEN legal men foregather with the laity in Scotland, they commonly set out a very vital point in Scots Law by telling the story of the music hall comedienne who gave a few rowdy students 'in charge'. They had ribbed her, perhaps a little over the score, at an extra-mural occasion. Reflecting in a calmer moment that the publicity might be damaging, more so since she aped a good natured, ebullient type in public, she asked that the charge be withdrawn. Confronted with the Procurator Fiscal, she was shocked when he boomed: 'Wumman, ye shairly dinna think that the Law of Scotland, in a' its majeestie, is stertit and stoppit at the blink o' a play actress?' As a matter of fact, the understanding man had already decided not to make a case, on the ground that *de minimis non curat lex*.

The point is that in Scotland the criminal law moves or stays solely at the discretion of the Crown, that is to say, the Scottish Crown. On the basis of the ascertained and assessed facts and circumstances, the decision to prosecute or not remains with the Lord Advocate, or his deputed agents, among them the local Procurators Fiscal. A private person may lodge a complaint. But he cannot make a formal charge and mount a case, as he can in England, even to the extent of murder.

Take the matter of the famous 'reiving' (lifting) of that Stone of Destiny which is presently held by the Dean and Chapter of Westminster Abbey against the spirit, if not the actual written terms of the main instrument of the Treaty of Northampton of 1328. The Glasgow students who did the job were soon well known. They left a trail of clues, and it was clear that they had burgled the Abbey under cover of darkness. But in the interest of the English public, the tricky business was shouldered on to the law of Scotland. No formal charge was ever made. It was held that the public weal was served by keeping quiet about the whole thing. The English public interest did not come off so well in the case of the Russian discus thrower, a certain Nina, who was alleged to have lifted some hats from a London store. Though the heavens fell, the English courts had to be set in motion at the word, as one gathers, of the shop people.

Actually, many, indeed most, of those 'smart work by the police' and 'proceedings in court' programmes that appear on television and are relayed to Scotland are quite foreign to the philosophy, principles and practice of Scots Law. For example, it ordinarily takes at least two witnesses to swear to a point of evidence in Scotland. As motorists and others from the south have timeously found out, that means that, failing other corroboration, it takes two policemen to make a charge stick. That in turn largely explains why the Scottish 'polis' go about in pairs. It is not so much that they need protection, as some suppose, as that the law requires doubly strengthened evidence. Since two witnesses can be cross-examined to any express point, that in turn means that true justice has all the better chance of being upheld.

To the further confusion of such script writers as want to pass muster in Scotland, adults cannot generally be put on probation there. Nor are there any Coroner's Courts nor public appearances before magistrates before a case goes to actual trial. If the Lord Advocate's man, normally the local Procurator Fiscal, is privately convinced, upon enquiry, that there is nothing fishy about an apparently unnatural death, he may authorise a death certificate without more ado. And it is up to him to assess whether or not there is a *prima facie* criminal case. Another prerogative of the Lord Advocate is that he alone determines the gravity of a case and the place of trial in the High Court or the Sheriff Court, with a jury, or before a Sheriff without a jury.

So it goes throughout the whole book. The 'phoney' marriage and its amusing consequences twenty years later, a favourite device of English playwrights and film scripters, does not make legal sense in Scotland. A marriage by 'habit and repute', and with or without the exhibition of a ring, is as binding in Scotland as the more ceremonial variety. That goes to the point that the offspring cannot be cut off with a shilling or less, as can be done in England. Based on this, the estranged son of a deceased nobleman recently found to his surprise that as he fell into the title, he also came by a good part of the family fortune.

One cannot of course go into all the differences between Scottish and English legal doctrine, practice and procedure in a brief commentary such as this. But it might be useful to trace out the course of a criminal trial in Scotland.

Once a suspect is cautioned and held, and any voluntary statements are noted, the job of the police with respect to him personally is virtually over. They cannot carry on with a 'third degree' grilling, in hope of extracting a confession, or other possibly incriminating evidence.

There is thereafter no public examination before magistrates, as in England. All the enquiries are conducted officially and confidentially. A decision to proceed or not then rests, as said, with the Lord Advocate's department.

The full terms of an indictment must be served to the prisoner, together with all the main relevancies which the Crown officers may seek to prove. The prisoner may examine all prospective productions and lists of witnesses. And he may call on the help of a solicitor and advocate to prepare a defence.

As several newspapers printed in Scotland, though hardly native because of that, have learned to their cost, the first a jury, or the public, is allowed to hear about the substantial reputed facts is when the prisoner appears in open court to become an accused and stand his trial.

In court, the prosecutor cannot open with an address to the jury, as he can in England. The evidence is led right away, on the principle that it should build up, of itself, into a case. While the Crown must stick close to its brief, the accused is allowed very considerable latitude. He may procure other witnesses during the course of the proceedings. On the side of the law, great care is taken to see that all the evidence has been properly obtained and is admissible. The Scottish judges are very jealous and zealous about this.

The accused may elect to conduct his own defence, as did the mass murderer Peter Manual, when his trial was already well under way. After the final address of the prosecutor, the last word goes to the accused.

Contrary to the required unanimity in England, a Scottish jury may reach a verdict by a majority. That degree of self perjury, with one soul searching juryman finally persuading all the rest to his mind, which has been the basis of several film dramas, is obviated in Scotland. Nor need a Scottish jury resolve its conflicts of opinion to bring a prompt end to its deliberations in time for trains or dinner. Finally a Scottish jury may depart from the alternatives of 'Guilty' or 'Not Guilty' and return a finding of 'Not Proven'.

Post finally, costs in criminal cases fall to the Crown. That is on the score that it is only right that the State should pay for the proceedings which it itself institutes. There is thus no question of a person being declared innocent, and yet mulcted, as can happen in England.

Touching on that very Scottish verdict of 'Not Proven', or, as some say, 'We know you did it, but can't prove it, so don't do it again, or else . . .' it so happens that that was, in a way, a backhanded present from England. During the 'Killing Times' in the latter half of the seventeenth century, when the Stewarts tried to set up Episcopacy and Bishops in Scotland by force of English arms, Scottish juries became more and more reluctant to send recalcitrant Presbyterians to the block, the firing squad or the hangman.

The word 'Guilty' stuck in their throats. At the worst they could not be prevailed upon to do more than answer the question, 'Are the facts proven or not proven?' In happier times the 'Proven' verdict remained to confound English legal logic, but to comfort Scottish reason and justice.

Indeed, the main body of Scots Law, if forged by Scottish hammers, was very largely worked to shape against English anvils. When it emerged in the twelfth century, it was mainly Anglo-Norman law, laced with some Canon and Roman law, on a stratum of ancient Celtic custom. Doubtless it was the Celtic influence that led to the enactment, as long ago as 1288, that maiden ladies of 'both highe and lowe estait' might bespeak prospective husbands in Leap Years.

During the Wars of Independence, such Scots law as was written moved away from the southern model, and then parted completely. Scottish jurists and students abandoned the Oxford 'schools' and thronged to Bologna and Pisa, Paris and Orleans, Leyden and Utrecht. A good deal of Continental Roman law thus came to be written into the Scottish law books. Away back in 1424, poor litigants were given free legal aid, as they still are in criminal cases. While feudal law remained, and still persists in form to this day, strictly English law completely vanished from the land. As is witnessed by the numerous legal terms and quips in David Lindsay's remarkable *Thrie Estaitis*, law became a favourite theme among the literati. John the Commonweal laboured to St. Andrews 'for to seek law'.

For all the distractions of dynastic, political and religious strife, and the constant military and civil pressures from England, the Scots made a good selective choice of broad principles, praetorian equity, natural and Biblical justice, and put in a dash of ideal metaphysics. When they set up the Court of Session in 1532 to deal with civil actions, they defined its written procedure very precisely. The pleadings have to be exactly marshalled on either side. In 1573, centuries before the English came to the position, they adjudged desertion or that wilful non-cohabitation which is tantamount to desertion, a cause for divorce. Drawing from the Roman tradition, they traced a dividing line at puberty between pupil and minor, instead of classing, as is done by the English, all who are not full grown adults as infants.

Over the centuries, they framed a set of land laws, with all the heritable titles set out in order in the Register of Sasines (established in the seventeenth century) which came to be the envy of the world. Unfortunately, the formal feudalism on which these laws are based has come to be cumbersome in these modern times when property in land and buildings upon it is greatly fragmented. In Scotland it is easier to acquire a marketable title to a motor car, than to a built garage in which to keep it. But, on the whole, Scots Law as it has sprung from the soil, is good law and fair besides. And the remarkable thing is that it has continued to grow in its own way since James the Sixth went to England in 1603, and the Estates of Scotland adjourned in 1707.

It certainly did not look as if that would happen when Oliver Cromwell, after his snatch victory at Dunbar, dismissed the Court of Session, with all its works. But when he departed to the shades, the 'English' judges, with all their horses and men, were sent packing, and the whole system was put together again. Not long afterwards in 1681, the general body of Scots Law was codified by Lord Stair in his *Institutions*. That was just in time for its protection and indeed preservation by the Treaty of Union of

1707. To be sure, that safe playing was in the blithe expectation that it would soon merge with the preponderant English system by a natural process. Instead of that, it moved even farther apart. This divergence was marked by John Erskine's *Institutes* of the eighteenth century and Joseph Bell's *Commentaries* (concerned with mercantile law) of the nineteenth century.

Since then, the edifice has remained strong and stable, though showing some cracks in its outer fabric, through the constant undermining of generations of Parliamentary draughtsmen at Westminster, who know and will no better. These fissures may be sealed by a new restatement which is now under preparation by the Scottish Universities Law Institute. Bearing on this, it may be said that, contrary to what obtains in England, the teaching of law in Scotland is in the province of the long established seats of learning. Every member of the Faculty of Advocates must have passed out through their portals with a parchment. There is no question of getting into the profession mainly by eating, as pretendent barristers do in England, a number of dinners at a common table. Lawyers in Scotland, from the old days, must be men of broad, and, at the same time, of narrow learning.

Touching on the governance of law, the juridical system in Scotland is topped and given very considerable dignity by the Senators of the College of Justice, each one now a Lord for life. James Boswell who hung so much on the words of Dr. Samuel Johnson did not always explain to the English, and even less to the Germans, that his father was not a baron, but a Law Lord. On the other hand, when Lord 'Cromac' arrived at an hotel to occupy a double room with Mrs. 'Carshuggle', he had to explain or risk a great raising of eyebrows. Hence the entitlement, since 1905, of each Senator's wife, as a Lady.

In maroon robes, the Senators assemble under their Lord President, as Lords in Council of the Court of Session. This deals with civil cases and sits only in Edinburgh. The Outer House judges cases brought to it. The two Divisions of the Inner House, headed respectively by the Lord President and the Lord Justice Clerk are mostly concerned with appeals.

In gowns of scarlet and white, the same Senators hold court as Lords Commissioner of the High Court of Justiciary under the Lord Justice General, he being the Lord President with the same change of raiment. This court convenes in Edinburgh for local trials or appeals. Otherwise, it travels round the cities and big towns, as occasion demands. It stems from the time when the Justiciar of Scotland acted for the King in all matters of justice.

Appeals against High Court decisions go to the Court of Criminal Appeal, an augmented sitting of the High Court of Justiciary itself. Beyond that there is no further recourse. Since 1926, Scotland has enjoyed complete self determination in one department, the administration of criminal law.

The executive side of the law is the business of the Lord Advocate. From the Crown Office in Edinburgh he acts through Deputes and Procurators Fiscal in the various sheriffdoms.

The Sheriffs Principal and their Deputes and Substitutes are the field officers of the Scottish law. Their status roughly matches that of an English County Court judge. But their duties are as various as in the days when the 'shire reeves' (of English derivation) were both governors and judges.

All in the day's work, Scottish sheriffs deal with civil actions, act as electoral returning officers, see to the swearing and recording of civil marriages, and give crime its deserts. But unlike the wild Western lawman, they carry no gun. Nor can they give anyone the rope. Their maximum sentence is up to two years in prison. They handle a great deal of work which would go to petty or quarter sessions in England and, at the same time, decide many cases that would go to the High Court in that country.

There have been Justices of the Peace in Scotland since 1587. But the office is not really indigenous and is still of small importance, being confined to minor courts in the county areas.

Most of the court work in burghs falls to Baillies, chosen from the elected Council. They have much the same standing as Aldermen in England. There are a few stipendiary or paid magistrates in the large cities. In the local courts, the Procurator Fiscal acts for the Crown.

The genius of Scots law is that it derives the greatest number of judgments from the smallest number of general principles by using the fewest number of legal tools. Hence the quick-change artistry of the lordly Senators and the versatility of the Sheriffs. As variegated in outward pattern as the native tartan, Scots law is as truly functional and matching to all purposes, as a web of that cloth.

It has its own philosophy and procedure about marriage,

divorce, births, wills, succession, reparation, contracts, damage and property, as well as about crime. And it has its own nomenclature and language. The 'tort' or actionable wrong in England is a 'delict' in Scotland. The English 'alimony' is not only 'aliment' but rather differently based and calculated. As few newspapers in Scotland seem aware, there is no 'arson' in Scotland but only 'incendiarism' or 'fire raising'. A person can change his name in Scotland without the formality of what the English call a 'deed poll'. At the same time, a married woman can stick to her maiden style, hence the Margaret Windsor or Jones of the Scottish courts. There is indeed a lot more to Scots Law than 'hamesucken', the double crime of assaulting, or 'socking', a person in his own house.

Naturally, if the English courts produced their 'hanging judge' Jeffreys, the Scots went one better with that Braxfield who liked to roar at unfortunates: 'Ye'll be nane the waur (none the worse) o' a hangin'.' But justice being served well in Scotland, he himself was dressed for hanging in the end. At his final 'cisting' (coffining) the undertaker drew a length of rope from his pocket, hitched it into a noose, and put it round his neck. He then shouted to the corpse: 'Monie a ane hae ye hangit, ye auld sinner, noo ye're hangit yersel', hoo dae ye like it, ye auld deevil?'

Perhaps many of the Scots judges, from the poverty of their origin, had a by-ordinary touching regard for property. It was Eskgrove who delivered this judgment on a tailor: 'Aye, no' only did ye thrust, propel or push the knife through the sodger's belly, and thus did murder him, but through his belt, which was his Majeesty's property.... Ye'll be hangit.' It was the same ardent who thundered at two housebreakers who assaulted and robbed Sir James Colquhoun in his own house at Luss: 'All this ye did, and God preserve us! Jist when Sir James was sitten doon at his denner ... Ye'll be hangit.' He obviously took a serious view of 'hamesuckin'.

In one field, however, the writ of Scots Law does not run in Scotland. That concerns Scottish service men, even in their own country. There, the English law of the Army Acts applies. But bearing in mind that Scots Law has continued to strengthen since the Estates of Scotland were adjourned *sine die* in 1707, that may not always be the case.

CHAPTER FIVE

THE KIRK OF SCOTLAND

NOT long ago it came out from the General Assembly of the Church of Scotland that the sessions and presbyteries of the Kirk might give their minds, and very tentatively, to the possible erection of titular bishops. This was to be in aid of closer communion with the Church of England, with its order of episcopacy. The stir which followed penetrated into every corner of the country. Among the multitude which enveighed mightily against the very idea, was a University professor, well known for his material views. A colleague mildly remarked in the refectory: 'What are you fashed about, you're the best part of an atheist?' But the reply came hot and strong: 'That's right enough, but a Presbyterian atheist.'

The feeling for the Presbyterian Kirk is in fact very deeply implanted in the Scottish conscience. It moves many who never set foot in a church from one year's end to the other. Though they may not know one tenet, doctrine or creed from another, in any real theological sense, Scots abroad generally go well out of their way to stick to the 'auld Kirk'. To do otherwise amounts to apostacy and a rank denial of nationality. South settling politicians who for form's sake move into the Church of England, with its 'peenies' (pinafores), put themselves right out of the pale. The feeling is so warm that the national tipple is commonly called, by way of the highest recommendation, a 'drap o' the Auld Kirk'! And like the beadle, the minister is the butt of whole books of friendly stories quite different in content and character from those directed at English vergers and vicars.

Always a sermon taster, it was a Glasgow beadle who described the sermon of a country minister as 'a hummel-bummel o' guid coorse countra' wark'. Always a man of dignity it was a rustic beadle who counselled a Glasgow student on pulpit duty: 'Jist you follow me, when ah tak up the Buik, but at a respectfu' distance like.' It was a Morayshire minister who intoned with bowed head: 'Oh Lord, we pray for the Prince of Wales, and if all we hear of him be true, he much needs our prayers, and, O Lord, bless our polisman, for he also, after a sort, is a servant of thine.' In short, the Kirk of Scotland if lacking in dignitaries, is very strong on human dignity. And for all the innovations that some people would like to push in, its staples remain the reading of the word, the extempore prayer and the marshalled sermon, with the comments that follow. 'Aye, there wis naethin' wrang wi' the text,' said the elder, laconically.

Taking in both communicant members and adherents, the established, though not state endowed Church of Scotland, enfolds about half of all adult Scots. It is thus far more national and embracing than the neighbouring Church of England. Moreover, it can always depend, when it comes to the bit, on strong support from the smaller Presbyterian bodies. These preaching churches, like the Reformed Presbyterians, the Free Presbyterians, the United Free Church and the Free Church of Scotland (the 'Wee Frees') are much stronger in numbers and even more in influence than their communion rolls would imply. Strongly evangelical, they take their faith very seriously. It is thus not unusual for adherents and regular attenders, postponing the day when they must depart from the profane to be with the elect, to put off entering into full membership until quite late in life.

Indeed, in some of the congregations in the Western Isles, the adherents far outnumber the full church members. For these churches there is no question of any perfunctory membership, so that their attendance record actually beats that of the disciplined, as to outward duties, Roman Catholic church. The other free (in the English sense) churches, like the Methodists, Baptists and Congregationalists are also strongly represented in Scotland and equally austere. And together with various apostolic churches, there are numerous gatherings of Brethren, and of course, the Salvation Army. Unlike the case in England, these smaller bodies are by no means limited to folk of limited means but embody quite a number of people of substance.

The native Episcopal Church in Scotland, though Anglican in form, and thus commonly called the 'English church', tends to be low in ceremony. Its main seats are in the north-east and for the rest among the gentility who like order and circumstance. Incidentally the Episcopal churches in North America drew more from Aberdeen than from Canterbury. Where this church is more evident, its members are often called 'Piskies'.

Oddly enough, as it may seem to the outsider, or perhaps not so oddly, one of the forces that has maintained the vitality of these very Protestant churches in modern times has been the rise of the Roman Catholic church. Save in a belt running across Scotland from the southern Hebrides to the Moray coast, that confession almost entirely withered away during the Reformation of four hundred years ago.

Since industrialism arrived, the Roman church has gained greatly on numbers, especially over the last hundred years. It was first substantially recruited by the armies of 'navigators' (navvies) brought from Ireland to cut the canals and lay the railways. Its renewed strength of around half a million adult members is almost entirely derived from continued immigration from that country. More recently, it has been reinforced in minor degree from Lithuania by entrants to the coal mines, from Italy by ice-cream merchants (cafés are commonly called 'Tally' shops) and still more recently from Poland, by disbanded servicemen. But since intermarriages and subsequent conversions are relatively infrequent, and very often act in the other direction, it now depends mainly on a higher than average birth rate.

Though it musters a fair number among the putative gentry, and the upper hierarchy which was set up again in 1878 is drawn almost exclusively from the small fraction of native stock, it is still regarded as an almost foreign and alien body over most of Scotland. With its main strength among the unskilled labouring classes in the cities, it is perhaps fair to say that it counts far less than its numbers would suggest, except in certain political and trade union departments. Partly by its stranger recruitment, partly by its own efforts, for instance its insistence on separate schools, and partly by its very sharp cleavage from the extremely non-sacerdotal Protestant churches, it is more isolated and apart than in England. In some districts, as in Glasgow and Lanarkshire, there is even a distinct Roman Catholic accent.

Contrariwise, its very presence tends to keep the Protestants, and indeed those who subscribe to no particular faith, very much on their toes. That in turn produces social and political pressures, still mostly undercover, which are beyond the understanding of the generality of the English.

To be sure, the Christian witness in Scotland is preponderantly evangelical and Presbyterian, as it is likely to remain. That is vouchsafed, not so much by the Treaty of Union of 1707, nor even by the seed of the Reformers, but by the enduring nature of the country and the shaping forces engendered by it. Presbyterianism fits the country like the glove the hand, and far more comfortably than Anglicanism in England or Roman Catholicism in southern Ireland.

The whole course of history amply shows that the Scots, from ancient days, have always heartened to simple forms of worship and order of church government. In spite of all the contrivances from inside, and pressures from outside, they have resisted sacerdotalism. Like the MacLeods, or the MacLeans, or any clan you like, who had 'boats of their own at the Flood' they have always essayed to be independent. Their first Christian church, seeded before Imperial Rome had stopped throwing saints to the lions, practised a simple pastoral faith. It was void of involved liturgy and free from a rigid diocesan organisation.

The first Sees were marked out and the first bishops set up in Roman style by the half Saxon, David the First.

He alienated such vast tracts and sums from the royal portion to build and endow abbeys, monasteries and churches as to be popularly canonised a 'Sair Sanct for the Croun'. Since the native clergy held to the ancient Celtic usages, he filled these houses with Englishmen, from orders already founded in the south. In the superstitious times, these incomers came to wield great power. But they were very soon Scotticised, so much so that they never yielded ecclesiastical authority to other than the Bishop of Rome. They denied the pretensions of York or Canterbury. To this day, the revived Roman Catholic church in Scotland depends directly from the Holy See. The Scottish prelates and clerics, many of whom were as much at home in the armed camp as by the altar, played a signal part during the Wars of Independence.

But their influence waned as their wealth grew, and as they became associated with that waxing France which came to regard Scotland more as an appanage than as an ally. The result was that the Lollard and Lutheran doctrines which came late to Scotland flourished all the more exceedingly. Even more than in neighbouring England, the Roman Catholic church suffered from its too great possessions. The outcome was that the Roman church and the French Alliance went down together in a successful rebellion of the growing Protestant 'congregation' against both Church and State.

Undoubtedly, as the prelates and their priests depended on French swords and lances, there was strong support for the Protestant cause from England. And looking to the wealth that had been shared out by the dissolution of the monasteries in that country, many of the Scottish nobles and gentry had their eyes more on possible material possessions, than on the niceties of doctrine. The great and abiding thing about the Reformation in Scotland was that it was carried out by the commonalty. There was no issue faked up by a monarch like Henry the Eighth of England who was 'Defender of the Faith' but who coveted more its treasures and its hierarchical rule. The Roman Catholic church was swept almost clean away out of its seats of power and the new Reformed Church achieved right away a modernity in organisation which was a wonder of the times, and is still a marvel to-day.

Events moved with extreme rapidity. On the 19th of July, 1560, three days after the contending French and English troops had left the country in terms of a treaty signed at Edinburgh on the 8th of that same month, the Reformers met in a service of thanksgiving at St. Giles' church. They then drew up a very evangelical Confession of Faith and Doctrine. This was put before the newly reassembled Estates on the 1st of August. After approval by the Lords of the Articles, who vetted new legislation, it was formally ratified by the Estates on the 24th of August, and thus became an Act of Parliament. The first General Assembly of the Reformed Church of Scotland then convened in a tiny kirk in Edinburgh on the 20th of December. Numbering no more than six ministers and thirty-four elders it boasted neither President nor Moderator.

This Assembly altered and abridged and then approved the first Book of Policy and Discipline concerning the new Church, which had been largely prepared by John Knox. Though submitted to the Privy Council the following January, this document was never formally ratified by the whole Estates. But being subscribed by a numerous company of leaders in the nation, it became charged with all the force of an enactment, though not possessing strictly legal sanction. Very significantly, about one-sixth of its whole content covered public education. Schools were to be established in every parish and colleges in every notable town. The three Universities were marked out for modernisation. From first to last the new Reformed Church was built and plainly furnished in about six months.

Much has been made in recent times, and in quarters that ought to know better (unless the intent is mere trouble making) of the 'dinging doon' of former handsome Roman churches by the Reformers. In fact the most of the destruction of the fabric of the religious houses loosely put to their account was the work of the English army which savaged the whole country from the Borders to Edinburgh in 1544. It hammered and fired all the abbeys. And the fell work was carried on by the English forces which carried out a slaughtering at Pinkie, just outside Edinburgh on a 'Black Saturday' in 1547. John Knox was then firmly chained to an oar in a French galley. Nor were the French troops, brought in to help the old order, very tender of Scottish stone and lime, churchly or otherwise.

Though strong for the clearing out of idols, John Knox and his fellows actually went well out of their way, and sometimes to their personal danger, to preserve the innocent buildings, as at Perth. As for the persons of the discomfited Roman Catholics, they were treated with a tolerance which was out of the world, for the turbulent times. The Reformers made no demur at Roman Catholic bishops continuing to sit in the Estates, at professors holding their chairs, as at Aberdeen and St. Andrews, and at ejected monks being paid a living portion for a generation, as at Arbroath. They themselves strangely appointed unregenerate clergy to read the scriptures and conduct the psalmody in the new Kirks and to teach in the new schools.

But as the Reformers cut clean away from the Roman system, as nowhere else in all Europe, there were others party to the far reaching changes. The Privy Council directed one-sixth of the Roman benefices to the Crown. On paper, it allotted a like fraction for the sustentation of the new ministers and the fulfilment of their educational and other plans. In the event the Crown, which collected all this revenue, held on to most of it. The remaining two-thirds were left peaceably with the actual titular holders, some of them being far from clerks in holy orders. The Reformed

Church fell into very little of the rich patrimony. However its grinding poverty proved to be its riches and strength. Its very modesty protected it.

That very pious Mary, Queen of Scots, who counted a mass as worth more than her crown, and eventually her head, was removed from the immediate scene. Most of the unruly Scottish nobles were then far too taken up with dynastic quarrels, and with what might happen to the broad lands and well filled treasury of the old church to worry overmuch about the organisation and doings of the new one.

The result was that the Reformed Church was thrown back on its own devices, the congregations and the preaching of the word. At the same time, it got leave to bring about a certain consolidating order. One imagines that it was regarded as being little pregnant with change as, say, a gathering of sober Jehovah's Witnesses to-day. A mere handful of quiet men did not seem to portend very much.

John Knox, who carried the banner for the Reformers, was by no means an all out iconoclast, save in the narrow sense of the word. He was strong for the paramount power of the General Assembly of the Kirk in spiritual matters and dead against any hierarchy of superior clergy leaning on the state. But just before he died in 1572, he was prepared to put up with the General Assembly's approval of administrative bishops. These were to rank as superintendents and be subject to itself. The mere name did not worry him at all, as all in communion with the church are held to be 'bishops', busy with the good work. As things turned out this, quite unwittingly, was one of the best of good offices for the Reformed Church.

The nobles and gentry, seeing their chance, pulled the numerous strings which were still in their hands. With the office apparently approved and free from suspicion, they managed to get tame clerics appointed to many of the continuing benefices, as straw dignitaries. Making private deals with these 'tulchans', as they were called from their familiar likeness to calves' skins stuffed with straw to induce unsuspecting cows to give milk, they then made away with the great bulk of the revenues of the former church which had not yet been directly appropriated. That put them financially, and eventually with their arms, against 'bishops' and by that chance on the side of the Reformers. When times changed and the new church had come to a Presbyterian and very egalitarian polity, the hungry nobles and gentry could not afford, in the exact sense, to oppose it.

This was one of these accidents which sometimes open the way for the right man and give an odd twist to the general rules of national ecology. Like Lenin, who was passed in a sealed train to broken but not yet revolutionary Russia, that man was Andrew Melville. He, and not John Knox, was the main architect of the Presbyterian Church of Scotland which stands and flourishes to-day. He was a profound scholar who, after many years in France, returned to shape Glasgow University, and, in due course, to put the new church in his native land on a firm and sure foundation.

Denouncing prelatic bishops and all their works as unscriptural, he stood by the doctrine of all being bishops in absolute parity in the ministry, and of absolute freedom from state control.

The Scots had always been in the habit of giving their kings the edge of their tongue. To his very face in his own palace at Falkland, Andrew Melville told James the Sixth : 'Thair is twa Kings and twa Kingdomes in Scotland. Thair is Chryst Jesus the King, and his Kingdome the Kirk, whase subject King James the Saxt is, and of whase Kingdome nocht a king, nor a lord, nor a heid, bot a member . . .'

Melville persuaded the General Assembly to set up district Presbyteries. Moving in between the individual Kirk Sessions and the provincial Synods, these took over the administration of an undefined and varying number of kirks or parishes. They embodied both lay elders and ministers.

This apparently innocent innovation proved to be of great moment. It provided a corporate body which took over the sphere of the Knoxian superintendents. Even more significantly, it erased the old diocesan boundaries. When the new system settled in, it was going to be as difficult to change it back again as, say, Napoleon's new order in France.

Considering the social and political arrangements of the times, the stepped up hierarchy of Sessions, Presbyteries, Synods and the General Assembly with their essential democracy and with the Presbyteries giving strength at the core, was centuries in advance of the age. There was nothing like it in politics for hundreds of years.

Fortunately, it got leave to bed down solidly. Those who might have opposed it tooth and nail, had they grasped what it meant, were otherwise engaged with their own schemes of advancement. Very naturally, the unique new church system did not match the 'Divine Right' ideas of James the Sixth. He did not like being called 'God's silly vassal'. Before he moved off to England he contrived to get titular bishops re-erected and to push the General Assembly into the background. But, wise man knowing his Scots, he did not interfere with the lower courts, and the Presbyteries carried on. Nor did he attempt to re-impose a full bodied liturgy. And even if it meant not a little backstairs intrigue and gerrymandering, he was always at pains to get paper approval for his moves.

His descendants in England were not so canny. Egged on by the suppliant and compliant place seekers around them, they felt strongly in their kingly powers. Without reckoning what had happened, they sought to saddle Scotland with a full blown episcopate, complete with liturgy and very expensive grandeur. This time they met head-on opposition. This came from more than the devout Presbyterians who took their faith seriously. It also came from the nobles, lairds and burgh councils. These people had nothing againt empty and inexpensive church titles, rather the opposite. But they were firmly against giving up the former church revenues and lands which had come their way to provide for lordly ecclesiastical dignitaries. That was hitting them on their money bags, where it really hurt. The old 'tulchan' bishops were the ghosts at their tables.

The result was the 'Bishops Wars', the beheading of Charles the First (he was given up to Cromwellian justice by the Scots), the infamy of Charles the Second, the flight of James the Seventh and Second and the downfall of the Stewarts. And the Presbyterian Kirk of Scotland assuredly would not have been as firmly founded had it been worldly about possessions at the start.

The Presbyterian order was specifically protected by special enactment at the time of the Treaty of Union of 1707. To this day the High Commissioner who posts up from London to represent the Crown at the yearly deliberations of the General Assembly has to be content to convey his greetings from the gallery. Unless he is also sent by a Kirk Session, he is no more than a visitor.

Some say that the Scots sold their Parliament to preserve their Kirk. Human nature being like that, it may well be supposed that there have always been those who would willingly dispose of the Kirk for some other consideration, possibly personal advancement. But the structure was, and remains, too firmly founded and braced to be easily shifted. It has of course been subject to external pressures. The London Government for instance denied to the parishes the right to choose and elect their own ministers. In 1711 it transferred patronage to the local landed heritors. It has also been ruptured internally over lesser points of order and doctrine. Echoes of these disputes between Burghers and anti-Burghers, New Lichts and Auld Lichts, and Lifters and anti-Lifters will be found in the works of Robert Burns.

In the Disruption of 1843, it split apart on the issue of patronage. It was then that the Free Church of Scotland departed to be independent with its own General Assembly. To-day, of course, the cause of that breach has disappeared, as the main body is free again from outside control. Patronage was abolished in 1879. There have been too, here and there and from time to time, minor innovations in the form of worship. The main Church of Scotland has long since taken to choirs and to these church organs or 'kists o' whustles' that are still abjured by the smaller groups. But the Kirk of Scotland remains pretty well as Andrew Melville founded and built it so many years ago. It is still attached to sober Genevan gowns, a plain order of service and to the Presbyterian form of church government, definitely without 'bishops' or rather with everyone a bishop.

The General Assembly is still presided over by the rotating Moderator, who was first chosen at its eighth convention and who, on the completion of his office, retires to the common vineyard. The ministers know no other distinction than their academic titling. The elders, whose numbers swelled the first General Assembly, are still the main guardians of the continuing purity and missionary endeavours of the Kirk.

While considering itself part of the Universal or Catholic Church, the Kirk of Scotland completely and utterly rejects the pretensions of the Roman Papacy. It is not concerned with the passage of priestly powers by the laying on of hands. Repelling all civil dominion in matters of conscience, it is free to stand by its own teachings.

It celebrates only two Sacraments. These are that of the Lord's Supper, dispensed, not from an altar, but from a communion table, and consciously understood and accepted Baptism. It is thus perfectly at liberty, as often surprises the more liturgical and sacramental Anglicans, to recognise divorce and subsequent remarriage. That has been part of the Law of Scotland since the Reformation. Nor is infant christening any more than a token to the offering parent to bring it up in good faith and works.

A few years ago some of the English-owned newspapers were in complete ignorance of this when they made a great fuss about a Highland minister refusing to christen a child of one whom he took to be ungodly. They did not comprehend that, claiming no priestly powers, he denied nothing to the innocent infant.

It may be granted that the Kirk of Scotland though offering full fellowship to all, does not number all the Scottish nation on its rolls. Preferring to stick to their own more or less Anglican ways, the native Episcopalians have indeed stood outside the tributes to the green memory of the Reformation in Scotland four hundred years ago. And of course for the numerous Roman Catholics now within the country 1560 was a very Black year.

But, as it itself was made by the country, the firmly upstanding Kirk undoubtedly shapes the polity of the whole nation. Scratch a Russian, and you get a Tartar. Scratch a true Scot, and you get a Presbyterian, though he may never darken a church door, nor put a coin in the plate.

Touching on this community the late Rev. James Barr used to relate with relish a story about the buirdly farmer who regularly came in from ten miles away to sit under him. 'Maister Broun, dae ye like ma sairmons?' enquired the minister, who had a good turn of Doric. 'Na, na, Maister Baur, it's no that, but ye maun be a guid meenister, fur ah ken your brither Tom, and man, he has a rare schule o' buists' (a good herd of cows).

CHAPTER SIX

THE SCHOOLS OF SCOTLAND

WHEN in the proper understanding company, a certain highly placed Scot likes to retail how he got well away in the Royal Air Force, right from the start. At his grooming interview for a commission, he was asked to estimate the distance from a window to a distant tree. 'About three hundred yards,' he answered pat. So it proved to be, within a few feet. Pressed to explain how he came by such exactitude, he volunteered : 'Well, I can drive a golf ball just short of three hundred yards, but I could barely land it by that tree.'

His acceptance was clinched when, to the searching and fateful question, 'Education?' he boldly replied: 'Auchtermutchkin Public.' His inquisitors could not place his accent. Nor did they know that, as everyone in most parts of Scotland can play golf for a few guineas a year, practically every boy goes to a real public school; that is to say, he attends a day school open to all, and generally co-educational. Some of these schools, notably in Glasgow and Edinburgh, are now fairly selective. But the broad pattern is made by the 'Schoolboy, with his satchel, and shining morning face, creeping like a snail, unwillingly to school'. That goes as well for the schoolgirl.

There are, of course, a few residential schools that ape the English style. These are not, however, an essential, far less a key part of the system. Indeed the boys, even when dressed in the kilt for walking out, as some affect, look and certainly sound foreign to the scene. Yet, right enough, the English type so-called 'public school' in Scotland, in conjunction with the 'Real MacKay' in England, has played a signal role in maintaining the equality of the Scottish mode. They separate out and neutralise those top seeking fractions in society that would otherwise scum and sour the plain mix beneath. That is because the 'public school accent'

49

which marks a lad out for preferment in England tends merely to set him apart in Scotland. Among the commonalty, it is not adjudged a 'class' accent, but a stranger English one.

One recently met a works' manager with a good Scots name from a family well enough connected to get him the job, who was at pains to Scottify his tongue which had been Englished at a 'good school' in Scotland. His trouble was that the men continued to take him for a Sassenach, and thus, as a matter of course, an interloper and not up to much.

The old Scottish school system which has maintained its traditional philosophy unbroken, if not unchanged, from the twelfth century is far more ancient and enduring, as a going concern, than anything obtaining in England. As such, and apart altogether from tending to elide class accents, it has exercised a subtle influence in tempering those class attitudes which are the bane of England.

For instance, since the orthodoxy is for the pupil to go to the nearest reasonable school, the choice of establishment is thus more or less automatic, for the vast, and formative, majority in Scotland. This obviates, or at least smothers that sort of double snobbery, not only between 'public school' and day school but also between the various grades of 'public school', that characterises England. It is not that there are not plenty in Scotland who rather fancy a classy turn of speech. But it is not much good parading a class accent which is not commonly identified as such among those very people it is designed to impress. At any rate, Englishmen who have been in the armed services will have noticed that in Scottish formations there is no such great gulf between the tones of the officers and men as is general in English regiments.

To come to the point, the keystone of Scottish education is the ordinary public school. That is the local establishment, maintained by the rates and government grants, and, in odd cases, assisted by endowments and minor fees. Beyond the elementary stage, these real public schools are now divided into junior secondary and senior secondary grades. Many of them retain the old names of 'Academy', 'High School' or 'Grammar School'. The English division into secondary modern, secondary technical and grammar schools is foreign to Scotland. Incidentally, the great divide occurs after the 12-plus, not the 11-plus examination, as in England.

These apparently innocent but really fundamental differences derive, like practically everything else in Scotland, from the interplay of a long series of factors. Contrary to a common opinion, even north of the Border, public education in Scotland, as opposed to the teaching of clerics, did not begin with the Reformers. There were regular secular schools all over Scotland in the twelfth century when the University of Oxford in England was itself no more than the 'Schools'. As far north as Aberdeen, the boys were forbidden to speak in the vulgar tongue of the region 'but only in Latin, Greek, Hebrew, French and Gaelic'. Most of the Scottish burghs had grammar schools, leading to the higher learnings, centuries before the Reformers saw the light.

The Universities of St. Andrews (1411), Glasgow (1451) and Aberdeen (1494) were in fact founded by Papal Bulls. As early as 1496, in the time of that James the Fourth who was slain at Flodden, the Estates of Scotland enacted that all the barons, burgesses and freeholders should send their sons and heirs to school where they were to remain until they were 'competently grounded and have perfect Latin'. The leading Reformers were thus all grammar school boys and university men of quite a different educational cut from the poor friars who carried Lollardy through England. Andrew Melville was a profound scholar with a European reputation. George Buchanan was reputed the best Latinist in all Europe and as such taught the young Montaigne.

John Knox, though he never claimed profundity, was himself the product of Haddington grammar school and he certainly took classes at Glasgow University, and perhaps also at St. Andrews. As an educationalist he sought to improve on the already old school system. To that end he carried a motion through the first General Assembly of the Reformed (though still not Presbyterian) Church in 1560, providing that grammar schools teaching Latin should be set up in every single town, and preparatory schools in every parish. More remarkably, attendance was to be compulsory and financial help had to be given as of right, in needful cases. Scotland was indeed in enjoyment of the first truly modern educational system in all Europe.

Unfortunately, or perhaps in the long run by good fortune, the king, nobles, gentry and town burgesses made away with the lion's share of the wealth of the demoralised and dispossessed Roman church. For a long time, therefore, the Knoxian scheme could not,

by lack of means, be implemented in any major way. But it was at
length set going properly by one of the last Acts of the last independent Scottish Parliament. That was the famous and fruitful
Act for the Settling of Schools passed in 1696. It was then that the
village 'dominie' entered upon his great labour in bringing on the
rustic 'lads o' pairts'. He did that for a mere small fraction of the
passing riches of forty pounds a year enjoyed by the schoolmaster
in Goldsmith's 'Deserted Village'. For over a hundred years his
maximum salary ran to no more than 200 merks, or say less than
eleven guineas sterling.

In the meantime, two more Universities had been established,
both quite remarkable in their own way. In 1583, the city fathers
of Edinburgh set up the Town's College. This was the first civic
University in all Britain, if not the world. The continuing Town
Council still has a say in its governance. Then since King's College
in Aberdeen had moved no farther away from the Roman doctrines than to Episcopacy, Marischal College was endowed in that
same town in 1593 to serve the Presbyterian interest. That was at
a time when the simple ejection of dissidents was the rule in
England. The two colleges were merged in 1860, by the University Act of 1858. But the Aberdonians still like to recall, in a
friendly way, that time was when their city was as well provided
scholastically to suit all tastes as Oxford and Cambridge rolled
into one, and not in new 'red brick' but in old solid granite.

Accordingly, when the Estates of Scotland adjourned in 1707
to become a mere memory, the country had a unique scholastic
provision for a nation of around a million people. Now, all this is
not recounted just out of patriotic, 'wha's like us' zeal. There must
have been deep reasons for the early florescence of truly public
education in Scotland. And there must have been forces making
for the development of that broad-based philosophy, linking the
arts and the sciences, which is still beyond the grasp of the English
to-day. The proposition is that these reasons and forces were
exactly those which nurtured personal and regional independence
and which seeded and brought to strength the astonishingly democratic Presbyterian Kirk.

The corollary is that these native and natural influences, being
born from the country and not from the people who happened to
live in it, are still active and will remain so. Whatever individuals
or factions may think, say or do, the strong interests making for

conformity over all Britain are thus bound to be defeated in the long run.

The Kirk, while not accounting good works in themselves as an entrance qualification for heaven, none the less fostered personal and corporate well doing. It did not require to have the poor around it for the better exercise of the sweet virtue of charity. Allied to this, the very Scottish schooling system, though still ill provided in material terms, had a tremendous effect on the common mind, standing and living of the whole Scottish nation.

Nor need anyone, either south or north of the Border dub that as mere prim priggishness. The far from unworldly government of to-day has agreed that the survival of Great Britain as a world power will depend, more than on anything else, on moral fibre and on the fruitfulness of education.

Anyway, a mere fifty years after the Kirk won free from external buffeting and the schools obtained a promising provision, the physical scene in Scotland completely changed. The poor barren country which had been rich in nothing save surplus manpower, national pride, independence and learning, suddenly became a veritable hive of trading, industrial and cultural activity.

Edinburgh filled up with printing presses and came to be called the Athens of the North. Though the steam engine had yet to be made tolerably efficient, Glasgow became a thriving commercial and manufacturing centre. In 1750, Scotland mustered almost 16 per cent of the whole population of Britain, compared with 14 per cent a century before. That proportion, the highest ever reached, compares with the 13.75 per cent of the Goschen formula (on which the financial share-out between Scotland and England is said, erroneously, to be based) which was struck on the percentage of 1851, and with the 10.5 per cent of to-day.

The mighty advance, all along the line, is often attributed to the benefits springing from the political union with England, and, in particular, to the opening up of the former purely English colonies to Scottish trade.

However, since the English nation could also trench on the same developing trade, and with greater convenience, the reason for the unusual progress must logically be sought elsewhere. Samuel ('Self Help') Smiles, born in Haddington and himself a prime, if somewhat smug example of self improvement, opined that it was all a fruit of the greatly reinforced and better provided parish schools. They tapped and brought on an intelligent class of country people who would not otherwise have been able to make a start at the grammar schools in the towns. As Dr. Thomas Guthrie mentions in his autobiography, these schools, which had a very broad and deep curriculum, enabled the sons of poor and humble people to pull themselves up in life, without their feelings of self-respect and manly independence being sapped by charity.

The position and the potential remained quite different in England until very much later. There, the schools which had been set up by the Roman church to maintain the flow of tolerably lettered clerics had become the virtual preserve of the landed and moneyed classes. That had come about by a process of slow intrusion. When, rather late in the day, the nobles and squires of England came to feel that there might be, after all, something in reading and writing, they put their sons to the church schools. Since this was rather a favour, in so far as the lads were not destined for holy orders, they agreed to pay for the tuition. Thus, though there was never any decisive break, over the years what had been free public schools in England gradually turned into expensive and exclusive private educational mills. Largely thanks to the all-out Reformation, that sort of gradual metamorphosis never happened in Scotland. The whole system of schooling was put under entirely new management, as it were. And, of course, there was always the added advantage that the social classes that fancied sumptuary divisions were skimmed off down to England, where they felt much more at home.

It is a fact that most of the mechanical inventors who changed the face of Scotland, men like Andrew Meikle, farm machinery, James Watt, steam engines, John Rennie, level bridges, and Thomas Telford, bridges, roads, canals and docks, were country bred. They came from a class which, if not exactly poverty stricken, could not readily have made a start at the schools in the big towns. In England, James Brindley, a man of similar parts, lacking the chance of an early schooling, remained virtually illiterate all his life, and thus suffered in his work. In Scotland, James Watt, the instrument maker, was always completely at home, and without pretensions, with the professoriate of Glasgow University. In England, much later, Michael Faraday, the blacksmith's son, was always regarded, for all his commanding stature, as a sort of very clever, but none the less jumped up bottle washer. That was the attitude of the then ruling scholastics at the Royal Institution in London.

That essential freedom of recruitment and of attitude which sprang up naturally from the Scottish soil was carried on the wind to permeate the whole Scottish system of schooling. It still does, against all the pressures and encroachments from authority. As the Universities moved away from the old 'regents' who had taken students through the whole course, and became divided into faculties with resident professors, they remained gatherings of students, choosing their own teachers. In England, they remained authoritarian, with the students very much under the thumbs of their ruling masters. To this day the Rector (now indeed shorn of his Lordship), the titular head of Scottish Universities, is elevated by the votes of the undergraduates. In England, the Chancellor is erected by the graduates and the ruling professoriate. Certainly, what with government grants and the consequent growth of state authority, the Scottish University student is no longer quite the free agent that he once was. But he is still not reduced to that state of pupilage which characterises his English counterpart.

The Scots did not rest content with being the first to provide free parochial schools to feed the burgh grammar schools and in course the Universities. They were the first to recognise that not everybody wanted, or needed, a highly scholastic education based on the classics and rhetoric. To that end, they led the way in establishing 'academies'. These precursors of the so-called 'modern' schools were devoted to such everyday subjects as English, mathematics, science, living languages and the like. They did without the grammar school Latin which, for the simple reason that the higher teaching was done in that tongue, was at one time necessary for all aiming at a University. In backward England, Samuel Johnson's efforts to establish an 'academy' failed for lack of support; hence his tramp to London, with his star and almost only pupil, David Garrick.

The Scots were also the first to give University lectures in English, or what passed for it in Scotland. They thus very early on set course to resolve that Latin-or-no-Latin question which is still troubling the ivy grown Universities in England. On the other hand, they never made any sharp cleavage between the humanities and the sciences. As the name, 'Humanity', still appears above the door of the Latin lecture room, that above the portal of what the English call 'Physics' is still 'Natural Philosophy'. The Scots, tracing no distinct barrier, make rather a tautology of philosophy and science. After all, Albert Einstein arrived at his theory of relativity by philosophic reasoning.

Having built and furnished the main educational structure, the Scots then got busy with supporting outworks. They took to organising Sunday and evening schools. Unlike the Sabbath Schools of to-day, the original Sunday schools in Scotland were mainly secular. Like the evening schools, they brought on the artisan and mechanical classes, who had been missed by the regular schools in the country and burghs. The result was that, as early as 1780, when working people in London and over most of England were still without letters, illiteracy had almost entirely disappeared from Glasgow and from Scotland at large. (With the too rapid advent of industrialism the position deteriorated somewhat in later years.)

This spread of education had a tremendous effect on Scottish life. It gave such as Robert Burns a much wider reading public than he could have reached in England. It led to the founding of the Scottish Labour Party and, directly out of that, to the growth of the 'British' Labour Party. On the more strictly educational side, it gave a turn to technical and technological training which has endured to this very day.

To wit, when what is now the Royal College of Science and Technology (the oldest establishment of its kind in the world) was set up in 1796, in terms of the will of Professor John Anderson, his executors could proceed on the basis that working men students already commanded the elements of the three r's. They did not have to be herded into elementary classes for preliminary coaching.

At the same time, merchants, industrialists and men of standing generally were willing not only to lend financial support but also to be enlisted as governors. David Dale, the Glasgow mill owner, who actually started most of the things that are credited to his godson, Robert Owen, was far-sighted enough to subscribe twenty guineas for a ticket of admission 'during perpetuity'. His heirs, if they read this, may now claim free tuition.

The direct result of this is the paramount standing in Scotland of the big central technological institution, of university level, and still ruled by the customers, as it were. When the English at long length came to go in for craft and technical education, the aspiring working men had to be given a grip of their letters before they were fit to attend more or less formal lectures and demonstrations. Hence the key position of the municipal technical college in England. The distinction is so enduring that Scotland had to be given quite separate treatment in a recent White Paper on 'Technical Education'.

For the rest, the Scots, by the hands of David Stow, a young Glasgow merchant, were the first to run schools in pedagogy itself, for the training of teachers. They were also the first to establish 'black squad' chairs in Engineering, Naval Architecture and Technical Chemistry, as also the first to give university degrees in these subjects, at Glasgow University. The very first chair in Technical Chemistry was actually endowed at what is now the Royal College of Science and Technology by James (Paraffin) Young, but the degree is conferred by the nearby Glasgow University.

Yet, in spite of their early pioneering with academic (in the specific sense), technical and technological education, the Scots never believed that a scientist could do quite well enough without literary or other culture, or that a classicist need know nothing about the sciences, and be the better for it. Indeed, it became a common thing for a Scot to take a degree in Arts before going on to Medicine, Law, Science or even Engineering.

The general outcome was that when the Education Act of 1870 at long last provided for more or less uniform elementary schooling in England and Wales, the School Boards in Scotland took over what was in effect a going concern. The great bulk of Scottish children were already attending school. And very significantly, one out of 140, compared with one out of ten times that number in England was at a grammar school, high school or academy.

In the interval the English have certainly done a great deal to reduce the Scottish lead. They have done that partly by making positive advances and partly by forcing English notions on the Scots. For example, in 1918, simply because the ordinary schools in England were run on a county basis, the long pedigreed parish School Boards in Scotland were abolished in favour of county-wide Education Authorities. It was then that the denominational schools, mostly Roman Catholic but a few Episcopalian, were 'transferred' under public management. These schools were how-ever vested with every freedom to give religious instruction according to their own particular lights. Again following the English idea, in 1929 the Education Authorities, which had been separately elected, were done away with to make way for Educa-tion Committees of County Councils.

That move boded no good to Scottish education; since it co-incided with the growth of local politics, it delivered the schools in many areas to committees heavily weighted by councillors who in Knox's day, the dominie having done his best, would have 'been sent to some handicraft or some other profitable exercise'. It introduced a frame of mind which accounted the mere fabric of the buildings as being more important than the matter conveyed inside. In the matter of grants it pulled Scotland, which had a high proportion of secondary schools, and non-fee paying at that, down to the eleven-eightieths ratio of the Goschen formula. And, in the matter of promotion, it handed the teachers over to people many of whom could have done with their continued services.

More recently, since the second world war, Scottish education has again been made to suffer. In aid of tidy administration, big buildings, and central cooking, small country schools have been closed down by the score. Some districts, as in the Western Isles, have been swept clean of children during school times. And with the sharp shedding of the sheep from the goats at twelve, the old freedom of movement from one level of school to another has been stopped. As for the indispensable teachers, their status, espe-cially that of the men, has been so depressed that even with swollen classes many children get no more than part-time schooling. Out of English politics there has been, whether conscious or no, an effort to proletarianise Scottish schools as they never were in the past.

Still, for all the buffeting in these latter times, Scottish public schooling has managed to preserve its own philosophy against heavy assault. It is no accident that the output of graduates, in-cluding those in the higher technologies, is still at twice the English rate. Nor is it without moment that while English teachers are organised in the National Union of Teachers, Scottish pedagogues being mostly graduates (as they once *all* were) prefer the Educational Institute of Scotland. Nor is it a casual thing that the public school in Scotland is exactly what the name means. To be sure, the recent maltreatment of Scottish schooling will eventually find its own remedy. That is guaranteed by the very soil of the country.

CHAPTER SEVEN

THE GOVERNANCE OF SCOTLAND

'*An uair a thig righ ur, thig lagh ur,*' (when a new king comes, there comes a new law), said one Highlander. 'Well then,' said the other, 'if God and ourselves do not stop it, we will soon have it at home beside us.' They made this exchange when news at length came to Ross that sixteen peers and forty-five gentlemen and burghers had ridden south out of Scotland in 1707 to join the incorporating Parliament of Great Britain. Then they both agreed that *cha bheir lagh air eigin* (the law cannot go beyond necessity). That, as wise legislators have long since found out, and unwise ones denied to their cost, is a fundamental if laws are to be observed. One remembers, for example, the dead letter of the Prohibition laws in the United States.

The Union of the Crowns, of the Scots as a nation and of England as a land, in 1603 had brought both good and evil to Scotland. Among the cavalcade which took the road to the south with James the Sixth were many who went for the pickings, and could well be spared. The Londoners, who called them 'ragged Scots', were welcome to them. And in the long run even the evil redounded to the good of the country. Out of the Bishops Wars and the long endured 'Killing Times', Scots Law, the Kirk of Scotland and the schools of the land emerged as even more Scottish and firmly planted in the soil of the country.

When the Parliament of England, seeking above all else to deny a rallying ground in the north to the exiled Stewarts, bought up and presently swallowed the Estates of Scotland, the two countries were entirely different in atmosphere, social organisation and governance.

Nor need anyone be surprised at that. As the Gaels say: 'An inch off or on the nose of a man makes a great difference'. A mere five hundred feet or so on to the height of Ben Nevis would make a great difference to it and Lochaber. With that comparatively little topped on, less than the added height of a televison mast, the mountain would have a permanent snowcap and the makings of a glacier. The positional and topographical differences between the two countries had set the neighbouring nations far apart. In Scotland, for instance, there was no chain of all-powerful state administration which could be simply pulled to get immediate action at a distance.

In England, the *Curia Regis* or private King's Court of the feudal Norman times had come to be attended by a gathering of barons and their knightly tenants. Their main function was to make scutage (taxes on their holdings) acceptable. As taxation was broadened the convention was extended to include knights representing the counties. At length in 1265, when the monarch was a prisoner in the hands of Simon de Montfort, the latter called for the return of knights from the body of the counties and of two burgesses from every city and town. Years later the territorial knights and citizens were set apart in their own chamber, or at least at the far end of Westminster Hall. The reason for this division was that they were levied a lot more substantially than the barons, the knights or the prelates. They thus had a common interest in voicing grievances.

That was the beginning of the separation of the Parliament of England into the Lords and the Commons. In course of time, the king struggled with the nobles. These latter, in the days of their dominance wiped themselves out with a right good will in the War of the Roses. At length an alliance between the monarch and the shrivelled nobility was put at naught by the new order raised up and armed in the Commonwealth. Political power fell into the hands of the Parliament, that is, into the grip of an oligarchy.

The writ of the Crown, which had been tamed, brought to heel and made a gift of the Parliament of privilege, penetrated into almost every last corner of the country. There were no natural obstacles of any consequence to deny it.

In Scotland, on the other hand, events had taken a completely different turn. How different can be amply seen to-day in the wide gulf between the constitutional arrangements in the United States and Great Britain. The sharing of the power between the President and the Congress of that great country, with full execution going to the President and legislation to the Congress, is really a sort of fossilised version of what obtained in England (meaning that individual country) centuries ago.

Copying the Normans in the south, even to the name, the King of the Scots set up his own *Curia Regis*. This King's Court also drew round it a council which took on the name of Parliament.

The first assembly carrying that name was called by the king himself, that swithering John Baliol who came at the pleasure of Edward the First of England in 1292, and was bundled out ignominiously in 1296. Far from being concerned with the niceties of taxation, that Parliament forced Baliol to break with Edward and banished all Englishmen from the realm. By this time the Scottish burghs which, though feudal entities, had never been broken as were the towns in England, had long since come together in the Convention of Royal Burghs. That convention, which now includes ordinary towns, is one of the oldest representative bodies in the world. These burghs sent men to the Parliament called by Robert Bruce to the Abbey of Cambuskenneth in 1326.

The difference is that these citizens, not being belaboured by the heavy end of the financial stick, sat, and continued to sit, in the general body of the hall. Hence the meeting under one single roof of what came to be known as the Three Estates, the King, the Lords and the Commons. This body, with its inner Committee of the Articles to prepare its business, combined legislative, judicial and executive functions. Though its franchise was extended from time to time, the Estates never possessed, or even particularly sought that complete independence which was ultimately the aim of the English Parliament. That was for the simple reason that since real power remained in the hands of the nation at large the law could not go beyond its tether.

Even when the imported feudal scaffolding of rights and privileges had disappeared, save in name, the various elements in the nation, the monarch, nobility, gentry, burghers and commonalty, maintained their own positions. And of course in the Highlands and Islands, where feudalism never found soil to grow, the chiefs and their clansmen still kept watch and ward, as in the old days. There are naturally those, including many in Scotland, who, going on the retention of such legal terms as 'superior', 'rights of servitude' and 'feu duty' (originally the commutation in cash of an obligation to serve) make out that Scotland remained a truly feudal and thus backward country. They are as far from the mark as future historians would be if they centred a picture of everyday life in Britain to-day on the opening of Parliament or on a royal marriage. The gilded horse-drawn carriages, complete with out-riders, postillions and running footmen and the words of the monarch *le roi* (or *la reine*) *veult* are as far from real life as Cinderella.

Since the 'pruif o' the pudden's in the preein' (tasting) o' it', it may be adduced that villeinage died out in Scotland with the Wars of Independence, centuries before it withered in England. The common hind in the fields was never reduced to that miser-able state which, as Thorold Rogers amply sets out in his *Six Centuries of Work and Wages*, was the portion of his fellow in England.

A living example of that is the sturdy independence of the farm hand in Scotland to-day. There were no despairing peasants' revolts in Scotland, like those of Jack Cade and Wat Tyler in England. Nor were there ever any burgher wars. There were plenty of 'palace revolutions' and lots of bloodshed, but the for-malities of feudalism rested easy on the country and betokened no systematic class oppression. The best gauge of that is that the monarch never became known as other than King of the Scots and that the same people who denied him lordship over the land built free schools and put organised democracy into their Pres-byterian Kirk long before anything of the kind had been evolved in any other country.

If the Scots allowed their legislature to be carted off, just like that, and never carried their noisy tumults into armed resistance, as they had often done in the past, it was largely because they were in a confused quandary.

In the final analysis, they agreed to trade the banishing of the Stewarts, which concerned the English, for the safeguarding of the Presbyterian Kirk against external assaults, which was of moment to them. An 'Act for Securing the Protestant Religion and Presbyterian Church Government' took pride of place in the Treaty of Union and was separately ratified. The Law of Scot-land was similarly preserved in the body of the Treaty, and with it the rights and privileges of the ancient Royal Burghs. What the English got out of it was the settlement of the Succession of the Crown, its further limitation and the 'extinguishing the hopes of the pretended Prince of Wales, and all other Pretenders, and their open and secret Abettors'.

They also shouldered on to Scotland a good share of the strictly English National Debt, which was already very considerable. Since the Scots had no state debt that mattered, they were given £398,085 10s. as compensation for taking up the burden. Passing over this 'Equivalent', as it was called, had the smell of a real smart piece of horse trading on the part of the canny southerners.

Sixteen Scottish peers were given seats in the House of Lords. They are still balloted to that limited number by their fellows. (There is however no restriction on the new United Kingdom peers.) Forty-five members then fell to be elected to the House of Commons, as might be arranged. For the first time, the legislators from Scotland were thus kept apart, in classes.

Right away, the lack of civil service administrative machinery in Scotland posed a problem to the London Government. It appointed a Secretary of State to interpret and deal with Scottish affairs. For the rest, it resorted to titled Scots who might, as it supposed, be able to mould public opinion and wield power in the distant country. Sometimes it fell as far short of knowing who was who, and what was what, as was Rudolf Hess when he imagined that the Duke of Hamilton was a power in the land. The Secretary of State disappeared in 1725, and then, after a brief reappearance in 1742, utterly vanished in 1746, the year of Culloden. Thereafter, with the Stewarts finally out, Westminster paid scant attention to the handful of Scots in Parliament, and resorted more and more to 'management' from a distance.

For this it relied on such organs of administration as existed in Scotland, bodies like the Commissioners of Supply in the counties, and the very local Parochial Boards. Truth to tell, with the Kirk, the Laws, the Burghs and the schools protected by treaty, it could not interfere a great deal in the daily life of the people. When it did in the belief, as William Pitt opined, that it made no odds 'whether a man were rocked in his cradle on this or that side of the Tweed', it uniformly made a mess of it. But that merely served to breathe reviving life into the Scottish nation. For example, its culpable treatment of the Company of Scotland Trading to Africa and the Indies led to the disaster at Darien and stirred the Scottish nation to the core.

Many true born Scots took up arms against the Stewarts. But

the sale of Highland estates to English carpet baggers after the 1715 Rebellion, and the bloody suppression of the clans after the 1745 Rising roused the national spirit. And it greatly invigorated its muse. Completely unmindful of the fact that the Stewarts lost their base in Scotland, and eventually their crown, by interfering with the Kirk, the English regime brought a hornet's nest about its ears when, riding rough-shod through the Treaty of Union, it denied the right of the churches to choose their own ministers. The reintroduction of patronage in 1711 convulsed the best part of the Scottish nation.

Westminster landed into trouble again when, misjudging Scottish sympathy with the events then taking place in France, it moved against the native radicalism with main force. It might have been advised that old Lord Auchinleck, the eminently respectable father of James Boswell, and himself a pillar of the law, had voiced approval for Oliver Cromwell in that 'he gart kings ken there was a lith (crick) in their neck.' It might have appreciated the essential dichotomy of such as Robert Burns, who sent an eulogy egging on George Washington and bought guns from a lugger to send to the French in revolt, but also stood to arms against the prospect of invasion. Incidentally, the same poet, in a trenchant piece, dubbed the politicians who arranged the Union, 'sic a parcel o' rogues in a nation.'

However, these vexations, though sore enough, helped to keep the Scottish nation together during a time of great change. There were plenty of sober men who drank to 'the little gentleman in the black velvet coat', the mole that stumbled the horse and put an end to the life of King William. And it was not only Jacobites who raised their glasses to the 'king through the glass' or 'over the water'. After all, there was nothing like a threat from the now highly romanticised Stewarts to keep the Westminster boys in order.

In the meantime, with the conquest of the open sea, the march of science and the onset of industrialism, local government in Scotland had become outmoded. More or less closed and self-perpetuating incorporations of merchants and craftsmen looked after the affairs of the burghs; in the country, the landed heritors and kirk sessions saw to parish matters, mainly schools and poor relief. However new duties, quite other than dispensing local justice and keeping the springs of commerce well open, piled on apace, especially in the burghs. Some of these, like policing the precincts and scavenging the streets, were at first made the concern of separate Police Commissioners. Indeed, the first full-time policemen (who were mostly on night duty) laid aside their batons and lanterns, and took up their sweeping besoms (brushes) as time afforded. The time passed too when people were content to draw their water from common wells or bought it from 'caddies' who lumped it around like the Eastern water sellers of to-day. What might be called big 'public utility' jobs began to fall to the common cost of the towns. The limited resources of the Scottish burghs which had served well enough in former times became strained. The position was cracked when the general body of burgesses in Arbroath elected their own council in 1817 and when Aberdeen corporation went bankrupt that same year. All kinds of pending changes were brought about by the passage of the Reform Act of 1832, and of the Scottish Municipal Reform Act of 1833.

The new extended Parliamentary franchise became the basis for the regular election of Town Councils. Still more duties, like lighting, cleansing, paving, draining, water supply and public health were entrusted to these new Councils by the later Reform Act of 1862. Further enactments added to their powers and obligations. But the dogsbody Police Commissioners were not finally merged with the Councils until 1900.

In the rural parts, similar modernisations were carried out. In 1872, School Boards were set up in each parish (and in the burghs) to implement the new Education Act. Though this measure was revolutionary in England, it merely recognised the position that had long since been attained in Scotland. In 1878, the roads were put under partly elected trustees. In 1889, the old Commissioners of Supply gave way to elected County Councils. In 1893, Parish Councils took over the duties of the Parochial Boards. In the Highlands a very special problem had obtruded. The chiefs had taken to considering the clan lands their own, and become landlords. Many of them were completely Anglicised, as they remain to-day. There is hardly a so-called 'chief' in the north to-day who talks a word of Gaelic, far less commands a turn of decent broad Scots. Become very fond of the bawbees, they thought nothing of giving the former clansmen the gate to make way for sheep and deer. But once these Gaels had ceased to believe that it was all an obscure dispensation of providence, there were quite a few battles on the braes. At length they were given security of tenure by the Crofter Holdings Act of 1886. Under this charter, the Scottish Land Court, which has no parallel in England, sees to the equitable sharing of interests in the townships in the seven crofting counties. All these departures seemed to be devolutionary and democratising to some extent. But, saving perhaps the measures protecting the crofters, they were all suspiciously like the ready made English model. Indeed that is exactly what they were designed to be, for there is hardly any nation like the English for blithely taking for granted that what is good for them is also good for other folk.

To match this growing panoply of control, a Secretary for Scotland was again appointed, after a lapse of 140 years, in 1885. Showing the very junior position of Scotland in the English scheme of things, this did not become a senior Cabinet post, carrying a Secretaryship of State, until 1926. Shortly after that, the English majority at Westminster again had its way. Dead against the old Scottish tradition of local control, the School Boards had been all flung together in 1918 into county Education Authorities. Under the Local Government (Scotland) Act of 1929, these were submerged in the County Councils. The relative decay of Scottish education began in that year. At the same time the Parish Councils which, though of recent embodiment, had a long lineage, were destroyed.

The powers of the smaller burghs were cut down, but as a token of local control, strictly limited District Councils were set up within the jurisdiction of the County Council framework. Their powers barely go beyond parks for the young and graveyards for the old. It all amounted to domestic centralisation and to a weakening of that local spirit which had characterised Scottish local affairs down through the centuries. Supposed to be in aid of efficiency, they were really designed to remove the organs of local control out of reach of the general masses who were now demanding more of a say. Several of the 'Red' Clydesiders, James Maxton for one, achieved their first public office in the separately elected Education Authority.

In effect, the new system has denied participation to people like school teachers, who cannot get away from their work regularly for daytime meetings. At that same time, it has opened the way, especially in the industrial areas, to the entry, at local level,

of professional party politicians. Being recouped for loss of earn-
ings (in the County Councils) if they can prove they are in paid
jobs, a good many of these now live very largely by their offices. In
the same way, the Town Councils, especially in the cities, have
tended to become the preserve of people who can afford ample
time. That means, on the 'Labour' side, people like trade union
organisers and insurance agents.

With the increasing output of legislation at Westminster, it
became obvious that special consideration would have to be given
to the application of these measures to Scotland. Accordingly, in
1894, the House of Commons set up the Standing Committee on
Scottish Bills which is now commonly called the Scottish Grand
Committee. But it also developed the practice of weighting what
was supposed to be a Scottish committee with English members,
so as to keep its party balance in tune with that of the whole
House. Some of these pressed members are filled with anything
but good will for Scotland.

The Scottish Office, which now has its headquarters in Edinburgh, with a bureau in London, has also grown. It now takes in
the Home Department, the Department of Health (which includes Housing), the Department of Education, and the Department of Agriculture and Fisheries. These are overseen by the Secretary of State (a Cabinet member), a Minister of State and a number of Under-Secretaries. But between the lot of them they have
nothing whatever to do with the manifold and very manifest
activities in Scotland of the Defence Ministries, the Ministry of
Power, the Ministry of Transport and such like. Nor do they
supervise those ministries which are steadily increasing their hold
over local affairs, the Ministry of Labour and National Service
and the Board of Trade. In short, over the bulk of day-to-day
affairs, Scotland is ruled as a regional appanage.

Farther down the line, the North of Scotland Hydro Electric
Board and the South of Scotland Electricity Board have won a
certain amount of freedom in the conduct of their everyday
affairs. But the gas industry, the coal industry, transport, the railways and, through the Board of Trade, every productive industry
that matters, is under dominion from distant London. Quite
recently the Scottish Industrial Estates were put under even
tighter London control. That is to say, the clammy and sometimes
very dead hand of London rests very heavily on very large sections

of Scottish life and daily business. The very acute housing problem in the industrial areas in Scotland is almost wholly a product of English control. Its genesis lies in the cross purposes of London-framed rent restriction acts and the old Scottish rating system.

The imposition of English ideas and control, though less openly evident, is now far more wide, deep and insidious than in the managing days of the Duke of Argyll, Lord Bute or Viscount Melville (Henry Dundas). It is at the root of the decay of education, the parlous state of housing, the politicisation of local government and the chronic unemployment. Unemployment in Scotland has been at twice the prevailing English rate for forty years on end. The very dog licences which replenish the local rates in England, are filched away from Scotland to relieve the British Exchequer.

Certainly the London Government has mustered a very numerous corps of people with vested interests in the subjection of Scotland. These run from Conservatives who like nothing better than to touch the hem of a king's garment for whatever evil ails them, to Labour people who worship big organisations and aim to catch the dripping from the roast. But at the same time, it has taken the question of Home Rule for Scotland out of the realm of sentiment into that of severe and pressing need.

There is no question that, given freedom to 'gang her ain gait', Scotland disposes of the natural and human means to live and thrive again, and sumptuously.

CHAPTER EIGHT

THE SCIENCE AND WORK
OF SCOTLAND

'A YOUNG gentleman, one of my pupils ... observed to me that when a thermometer had been immersed in spirit of wine ...' William Cullen, Doctor of Medicine and the first lecturer in Chemistry at Glasgow University, then went on to say, in effect, in the one and only paper on the subject he ever put in print, that when the instrument was taken out and waved in the air the mercury always sank by two or three degrees. The observation, apparently innocent enough, proved to be one of the most, if not the most, fruitful in the whole history of the world. It heralded the Industrial Revolution.

To the day of his death, Cullen himself never fathomed the phenomenon. But his immediate successor, Joseph Black, also a Doctor of Medicine, conceived that an evaporating liquid, like boiling water, absorbs and stores away heat while changing its state. Without knowing anything about Black's theory of 'latent heat', millions throughout time have used their wind to cool their broth. But the great difference with James Watt, the instrument maker at Glasgow University, was that, on being put, by Black, in the way of understanding the absorption of heat by boiling water, and its rejection by condensing steam, he developed his new and vastly improved steam engine. This simple machine put cheap, massive and controllable power at the elbow of man for the first time. It then cut the whole history of the world clean in two.

As Dr. William Cullen postulated : 'It is always by the successive labours of Several that an art is brought to perfection ... The Case is, a second improved upon it, a third puts it in execution; and all claim the honour of the invention.' It was such a concatenation of labours, and even more so a linking of natural forces and circumstances that led straight to Watt's wonder working machine being put together at Glasgow in Scotland and at no other place on the face of the earth.

As one has seen, it was the position and framing of Scotland, the soil, the water and the winds that preserved the freedom of Scotland, both without and within. It was the same nature that led the people in the country to seek a simple faith, to contrive just laws and to add a well fortified mind to the strength of the arms which wielded the sword and spear.

But with a powerful neighbour in the south always ready to probe a weakness and to extend its dominion, all this might have gone for naught in the new times, save that the narrow waist of Scotland was not only a very odd configuration but also proved to be extremely well endowed.

East and west it is lapped by the deep sea. Easy land routes open to the north and to the south and England. When the ocean was mastered by the square-rigged ship and wheeled traffic became possible on land, this made for the development of commerce, both inside and out with the region.

The soil is rich, well watered and sheltered. When the Scots got leave to till their fields, they soon came to be very apt husbandmen. In fact, they led the way in what is called the Agricultural Revolution.

It was on these same fields that they then applied and bettered their chemical science, which came out of mathematics and medicine. Counting in no more than Colin MacLaurin of Glendaruel and John Napier of Merchiston, the Scots, for a very small nation, have contributed more to mathematics than the general world realises. Napier's system of logarithms are said to stand uniquely out of the body of the science like Rockall out of the Atlantic. As for their schools of medicine, they occupy a very large part of any history of the healing arts. It was from medicine and the surrounding fields that Joseph Black began the Chemical Revolution. The first proper chemical factory in the world was put up right in Glasgow.

Yet the commanding position won from the waterway, and from these green fields might have been lost, if the river Clyde, ages ago, had not turned in its course and broken its back in the middle of its run. 'Annan, Tweed and Clyde, rise a' oot o' the ae hillside, Tweed ran, Annan wan, but Clyde fell and broke her back ower Cora Linn.' It was in the deep gorge below Cora Linn that David Dale harnessed, right in the middle of Lanarkshire and well inland, enough water power to drive his great cotton mills. That is to say, the middle belt of Scotland was well away with the mechanical revolution before Watt's steam engine was fit to turn to real purpose. The planting of these mills, out of the fortuitous bounty of wild nature, clinched the industrial position of the valley of the Clyde and of the city of Glasgow.

Yet even this lead might have been whittled away, save that both coal and the makings of iron were found in plenty and together right on the spot. Not only that, these mineral riches were found very near the surface on the very banks of the rivers. The narrow region thus disposed both of the metal to make the machines and of the fuel to drive them. In England, of course, the coal and metal using industrial revolution forced a major shift in population from the agricultural south to the coal and iron ore fields of the north. Hence the makeshift appearance of the English mill towns. They were put up to house hands and make 'money out of muck'. Glasgow, for its part, came to combine the attributes of an ecclesiastical, scholastic, commercial, financial, manufacturing and metallurgical centre. No other city in Britain, and few if any in the world has ever boasted such manifold advantages.

However, considering that there are still plenty of places on the earth bursting with natural treasures, but deficient in the will to make use of them, the natural qualities of the odd strath running between Glasgow and Edinburgh might have availed little but for still another factor.

It so happened that Scotland had come to be peopled with a very peculiar race. As their elders sat in the same kirk pews, the children of all classes, gentry and ploughmen, merchants, craftsmen and day labourers all sat down on the same school benches. And as it was not out of the way for a poor man to rise by his own efforts, to gladden the heart of himself and Samuel Smiles, it was quite the done thing for men of landed fortune and title to engage in trade and industry.

The William Elphinstone who sold salt herrings to such profitable purpose out of Glasgow that the humble fare became known as 'Glasgow magistrates', and the other way about, was the son of a very aristocratic house. Incidentally, as a reminder of the not so distant time when the town had little else to market, the song of Glasgow Corporation, in convivial mood assembled, is *Caller Herrin'*. On the other hand, the Allan Glen who founded the famous school of that name was no more than a joiner. It was indeed in education that the natural democracy of the country was most evident. The encouragement of learning was such an ordinary matter of Presbyterian piety that it was nothing for a poor hind or a horny handed journeyman to take to his books.

From this, there were no Brahmins in the higher seats of learning. In fact they say that the first lectures other than in Latin at Glasgow University were not in English at all, but in very broad Scots. That in itself turned out to be a very important consideration. At an English University, James Watt would never have been on nodding, far less speaking terms with the dons. At Glasgow, he was on easy and everyday fellowship with the learned professoriate. The general result was that when Scotland lost her formal political freedom, she gained a larger freedom to get down to improving work. All classes put their minds and hands to the task. The particular outcome for James Watt was that he not only got a workable theory about heat from Professor Joseph Black, but also the loan of £1,000 to get ahead with doing something practical about it.

To be sure, since the fruitfulness of a nation is not seminated and in course germinated by its occasional very great men, but springs spontaneously from the genius of the general body, perhaps something more should be added to this story. To make a start somewhere, it so happened that in 1746, Alexander Dunlop, the newly appointed Professor of Oriental languages at Glasgow University was allowed preliminary leave of absence to act as tutor to a nobleman in Geneva. Knowing that his medical colleagues were greatly interested in putting some system into the teaching of the new chemistry, he proposed that the £30 saved from his deferred stipend should be devoted to equipping a laboratory. Adding another £22, the Senate raised the laboratory and appointed Dr. William Cullen, from Hamilton, as its first lecturer, at £20 a year.

A practical man, with a farming background, his father being factor to the Duke of Hamilton, Cullen, as well as traversing the then theories, set his students to experimental work. Fiddling about with a thermometer young Matthew Dobson (now revealed by name for the first time) noted the curiosity of the fall in the mercury when the instrument was taken out from a glass of alcoholic spirit of wine. Now, he might easily not have noticed the minor drop, except that Alexander Wilson had come from St. Andrews to settle in Glasgow. This Wilson, who afterwards became the first Professor of Astronomy at Glasgow, had a great width of interest and marvellous dexterity with his hands. Before Benjamin Franklin ever thought about kites in North America, he used the same means to raise thermometers into the air. He also founded the type that brought fame to the Glasgow printing works.

Alexander Wilson also made new style and very exactly calibrated thermometers that were rated the most perfect in the world. They had to be good for the cheapest cost the no small sum of one guinea. It was one of these Glasgow-made instruments that opened the way to Dobson's observation, to Cullen's comment and to Joseph Black's theory of Latent Heat. Even so, that notion might have been of no more than passing interest to the University mechanic James Watt, save for that infinitely curious and odd fellow, John Anderson, Professor of Natural Philosophy but more commonly called 'Jolly Jack Phosphorus'. Anderson, the same who willed the foundation of what is now the Royal College of Science and Technology, and that on a deficit of £55, came into a small model of a Newcomen atmospheric steam engine.

This model, which may be seen to-day in the corner of the Hunterian Museum at Glasgow University just would not run properly. It was accordingly sent back to London for attention. However, on hearing of this, Anderson ordered that the machine be brought right back. He maintained that James Watt, who had already done some exacting work in his small workshop by the University gate on some astronomical apparatus would be the man to effect the repairs. In fact there was nothing much wrong with the wee steam engine, except that the boiler was too small and could not maintain a head of vapour. But it was from working with the machine, in the light of what he had been told about latent heat by Dr. Joseph Black, that Watt arrived at the principle of separate condensing.

Even then, the chain of events might have been broken, to be welded together again very possibly at some other and distant place, if Black had not been the sort of Scots-reared professor to lend a mechanic £1,000 to address himself to the new idea. And it might have been sundered again, save that over at Kinneil, by Bo'ness on the Forth, John Roebuck was badly in need of some mechanical machinery to lift water out of his coal mines. Roebuck was a medical man turned engineer and entrepreneur. Pressed immediately with this necessity, Roebuck took over the debt and financed Watt's first and fateful patent : A new Method of Lessening the Consumption of Steam and Fuel in Fire Engines, January 9th, 1769 (No. 915).

The chain was indeed cracked and torn apart under impact from a bank crash which brought down Roebuck's many enterprises. Among many other things, he had started the first sulphuric plant in the world at Preston Pans about 1746. In passing, it may be remarked that that also sprang out of the Scottish fields. Something better than sour milk was needed to bleach the linen which was then a manufacturing staple in the country. Roebuck's two-thirds share in Watts' patent fell to his creditor, Matthew Boulton, far down in Birmingham. It was valued in the bankrupted inventory at exactly nothing. Though it still took some time, and a lot of Boulton's money to prove the practical merits of Watt's machine, it was very definitely a product of Scotland, and once going to purpose, it had a very immediate and fruitful application in the country.

The improved good-going steam engine was in fact as truly native to Scotland as the laws, the Kirk and the schools. It was just there, and nowhere else at the time, that the new style scientists got leave to breathe the free air. It was only there, in an ambience of enquiry and of free communion among all sorts of men, that the medical doctors were able to go from their apothecary mixtures to the chemistry of the fields, and the natural philosophy (physics) of the workshop and factory. Their enterprise derived not so much from their blood, as from the air around them. Bearing on this, it may as well be now revealed that the student, Matthew Dobson, was an Englishman, from Bolton. He died at Bath, no more known to fame, until now, than that he married a lady, Sussanah, who wrote books. And John Roebuck was also a southerner, who came like many more, to Scotland to better himself, and was welcome.

However, a great many other forces had to conspire together to make Scotland, not only the fount of world-shaking invention, but also the first powered workshop of the world. Quite as much as fruitful fields, coal, metal, power and even ideas, the life blood of commerce and industry is free flowing cash.

Fortunately, just before the Union, the Scots had taken time by the forelock, by establishing their own banking system, and had developed a natural, and indeed a national aptitude, for making the available, but very scarce, minted money spin out and work over-time. It was John Paterson, from Scotland, who showed the English the trick of lending cash to the Government, and then loaning the credit thus established to the generality. He was virtually the founder of the Bank of England which was set on foot in 1694. And it was of course another Scot, John Law, who tipped off the French how to get by with credit and paper money.

The Bank of Scotland which was founded under charter in 1695 (just in time) was, and remains, quite different in philosophy and practice from the Bank of England. Beyond being given a term of years to settle down, it never sought, nor was granted, a pernicious and enfeebling monopoly. It soon made full use of credit and paper money. And when it resorted to accepting and then seeking general deposits, to eke out its own provided capital, it ranged round branch banks to achieve a firm broad basis for its business. Like the other banks that came to compete with it, the Bank of Scotland paid special attention to the credit and cash needs of commerce and industry right from the start.

The British Linen Bank founded in 1746 indeed grew directly out of the linen business. And the Commercial Bank of Scotland was expressly organised in 1810 to serve the business community. The Scottish houses were in fact the first in the world to practise really modern banking. Nor was that due to the fortuitous assembly of money spinning talent. The Scots law of society was much more congenial to the development of company enterprise than the common law of England, which latter prohibited joint-stock enterprise in ordinary trading and manufacturing right until 1844. With its evaluation of moral character, the Presbyterian doctrine also favoured the typically Scottish 'cash credits', in effect overdrafts on personal security. These overdrafts were first issued by the Royal Bank of Scotland in 1728.

Then, of course, it was the proverbial 'every mickle maks a muckle' attitude that led the Scots to open the doors of the first savings bank in the world, at Ruthwell in Dumfriesshire, to gather in the odd silver and copper. With the increasing range and complexity of their financial business it was then natural that the Scots were also the first to make accountancy a profession on its own. The accountancy bodies incorporated in Edinburgh in 1853, and in Glasgow in 1855, were the first of their kind in the world, and they still command great prestige in the profession, all over the world. To this day the Scottish banks give readier, cheaper and better service than any commonly available in England.

Though some now have English connections, and some have recently merged within the country, the Scottish banks are still very much on their own and are strong in the management of their own fiduciary note issues. In 1826 they successfully held out against the London Government's proposal that all notes under £5 in value should be withdrawn. Consequently, until the Kaiser War, the Scots were the only people in Britain familiar with paper money.

With all this banking apparatus already well in the making it was not surprising that the Scots should lay out very carefully the first sizeable block of capital that ever came to their hands. That was the 'Equivalent' of £398,085 10s., paid over by the English, in return for the Scots, who had no significant state debt, shouldering a good whack of the already considerable burden carried in London.

Together with the accumulation of the beggarly £2,000 a year which had been promised by the London regime for the development of Scottish manufactures and fisheries, most of this 'Equivalent' went for the purposes of the 'Society of Improvers in the Knowledge of Agriculture' and the 'Trustees of Manufacture'. The Royal Bank of Scotland, incorporated under charter in 1727, actually grew out of the 'Equivalent Company' which was intimately concerned with these moves.

The first notable advances were made in the flax fields and in the associated linen industry. Very soon the Scots who started from scratch were abreast of, and shortly in front of, the English in agriculture. As anyone with the leisure to go into the history of agriculture will readily discern, they led the way in the application of mechanics and the new science to the fields.

This revolution on the land was a prerequisite for the pending surge forward in the factories. For example, it took such as

Andrew Meikle's mechanical threshing machine to release some of the numerous hands that had to be kept round the farmsteads for the rush of harvest work and to feed these people as they crowded into the towns. And it was mainly the fast developing linen industry that stimulated both the new chemistry and systematic iron working. In addition to the world's first sulphuric acid plant at Preston Pans, the first properly designed iron work at Carron grew out of the flax fields. In short course the increasing local demand for bleaching and processing chemicals, for fuel and for power, led to the growth of the heavy chemical (the first ever chemical factory was built in Glasgow in 1797 to make bleaching powder) and the coal mining trades.

It was of course from the coal industry, with its need for winding minerals and pumping water up from greater depths that James Watt got his first order for a working steam engine, some years before he teamed up with Matthew Boulton in Birmingham. Then it was from linen that the textile manufacturers took to spinning and weaving the new cotton which came from India. The first of the cotton factories was actually built at Rothesay on the Isle of Bute. The point is that while endeavours such as these were all disjointed and scattered in England, they all tied up into a neat parcel in the middle belt of Scotland, that is to say in the very part of the country that was already best served and most highly developed. The result was that Glasgow at one end and Edinburgh at the other became not only hives of industry but also, after their kind, centres of enquiry and nurseries of culture.

In Glasgow, Adam Smith wrote his *Enquiry into the Nature and Causes of the Wealth of Nations* while in more metaphysical Edinburgh David Hume set out his *Treatise on Human Nature*. At the same time, while the Edinburgh painters came to be very busy at their easels, two booksellers, Robert and Andrew Foulis, organised the first open art exhibitions and set going an Academy of the Fine Arts, nine years before the Royal Academy was ever thought of in populous London. More will be said about this abundant floriation of the arts in a following chapter.

Especially in and around Glasgow, it was not all plain and jolly sailing. The very lucrative tobacco trade with the Americans which that city built up became a casualty during the North American War of Independence.

However, the gap was presently more than amply bridged by

the cotton industry which then drew its fibres from the East. As few in England, and indeed not very many in Scotland, know, the West of Scotland built up and commanded the cotton trade, long before Lancashire made its mark in that business.

One weakness still remained. The local ironstone and coal, while handy, were not suited in quality to the methods of iron manufacture which were then usual. But the position was turned right round when James Beaumont Neilson introduced his famous 'hot blast'. The hitherto indifferent blackband ore and hard splint coal available in the waist of Scotland proved to be just the things for blowing up with hot air.

By about 1840, the narrow region was the leading and by far the cheapest producer of pig iron in all Britain, and indeed in the whole world. Around 1870, when the native ironstone workings, though still in the event productive for many a year ahead, none the less showed signs of eventual exhaustion, the Scots iron masters took the lead in reaching out to Spain for rich mineral. They balanced the extra cost of this by going in for the recovery of saleable by-products in a way that was not then possible in England. That was due to the technical fact that while the English blast furnace operators were put to using dry coke as a furnace fuel, the Scots were able to charge fat splint coal. Being also well provided with locally won refractories the area was thus extremely well set to turn out cast-iron products and also to convert pig iron into puddled wrought iron.

When inventors like Henry Bessemer and Charles Siemens in turn brought out new methods of making mild steel in quantity and cheaply, the valley of the Clyde was extremely well placed to take advantage of them. The Siemens furnace was actually based on earlier Scottish patents, filed by the Rev. Robert Stirling. The second open hearth furnace in the world was put into commission at Hallside, near Glasgow. It was this plethora of power producing and iron and steel making advantages that set in train the concerted move to metal working, engineering and the building of steel ships. Though the regional cotton industry was disrupted by the North American Civil War (as the tobacco business had been by the North American War of Independence) it was not lost to Lancashire, as many people ignorantly imagine. It was as good as handed over 'on a plate' for the simple reason that the Clydeside area could apply its financial, material and human resources to much better and more profitable purpose in the power and metal using trades.

In short, the pattern of industry which persists to this day was shaped, like the Kirk, the Law and the schools, by very native and very powerful ecological factors. That's not to say that Scotland came to depend, as is an all too common notion, on the 'black squad' trades. In point of fact the spread of industry over present day Scotland corresponds very closely to that over Great Britain at large. On top of that, Scotland is relatively much stronger than England in agriculture, fisheries and forestry. And of course the country dominates such specialities as whisky, fine woollens and seed potatoes, to name only a small selection. To be sure, taking in the whole range from farming and fishing, to the latest in atomic engineering, Scottish industry is extremely broadly based and well framed.

As it happens, it is that very strength that provides the key to understanding the industrial weaknesses, and the derived political stresses that now trouble the country.

During the long years when Scotland was palpably 'managed' from London, the natural material and human resources of the country were such that it hardly mattered where the seat of government lay. The native Scottish institutions all carried on rejoicing. The natural democracy arising from the very soil more than made up for the lack of English style local government organs. For years after the revolution in the fields and factories really got going, Scotland remained a vigorously developing pioneer country, always one jump ahead of the rest. The working man profited more from being able to 'write his own ticket', as it were, than from defensive trade organisations and a proliferation of councils.

There were beatings and bludgeonings here and there and doubtless a good deal of misery from time to time. But the population steadily increased and indeed at length had to be sustained by masses of common labour from Ireland. These were sure signs that common life was thriving.

Though the old condition of natural balance suited Scotland quite well, the importation of English-made local councils, all complete with an extended franchise, was doubtless in line with the times. But the fact remains that Scotland educated practically all her people, made a deep mark on letters and the arts, furnished her towns and achieved a very thriving economy, with world wide connections, before there was a single formally and popularly (in the real sense) elected council in the country.

The new system of local government presented to Scotland was, of course, accompanied by the growing participation of the London establishment in all manner of affairs. This inevitably meant increased taxation and added demands on the Scottish purse. Some of the money was returned but an increasing and very considerable amount remained in England. Yet for all this tribute, the healthy strength of the native Scottish economy was such that the average money income and the general standard of life remained higher in Scotland than in England during the whole of the nineteenth century. Moore's *Song of the Shirt* was very much a lay of comparatively poverty stricken and subsidised England. Even well into the twentieth century the scene was pictured by the Town Clerk of Glasgow as recently as 1915. In assessing his dictum it should be born in mind that, as Glasgow is, so also is much of the rest of Scotland.

'No city has rivalled,' he said, 'far less surpassed Glasgow, the commercial metropolis of Scotland. This has chiefly arisen from the city being 'cosmopolitan' in its commerce and manufactures . . .'

He then went on to retail the multifarious, and unrivalled manufacturing and commercial activities of the city which traded with every quarter of the globe and dealt in the products of every country.

Then he wound up in what may make surprising reading to many to-day : 'It hence appears, that while one branch of manufacture or trade may be dull, another may be prosperous. Accordingly, Glasgow does not feel any of these universal depressions which so frequently occur in places limited to one or two branches of manufacture or commerce . . .'

That view, which must be accepted as authoritative, was set out just forty-five years ago. Since then times have changed. The bustling city, and much of Scotland with it, has become subject to a certain wasting sickness. Since shortly after the end of the Kaiser War, worklessness in Scotland has remained, in good times and bad, at twice the English rate. Always a very significant pointer, the Scottish share of the British steel output which stood at no less than 23 per cent in 1920, has been halved. But the one thing that has continued to flourish has been growing inter-ference from England. Now, it may be said that the inability of Scotland to obtain a notional share of all these new industries that have grown up since 1920 is at the root of the trouble.

That, on the face of things, is true enough. The older trades that, out of the natural and contrived advantages offered by the country, came to be so heavily represented in Scotland, now make do with less labour, even when producing more, as some do. At the same time, the new activities, like motor car making, domestic engineering and electronics, which might have taken up the technological displacement, have tended to group in England, under pull of the same sort of locational benefits. On top of that, there is a marked tendency for more and more of the government's taxation money to be laid out in and around London. The general result is that that great city, with the so called Home Counties and the convenient Midlands, have scooped the new pool.

The upshot is that the now weakened Scottish economy can no longer carry, as it did for two hundred years without any visible marks of material hardship, the financial burden of too close incorporation with England. With the impetus of these agricul-tural and industrial revolutions which so favoured Scotland now gone, the country can no longer afford to send hundreds of mil-lions of pounds every year to England in virtual tribute. That is, as one now affirms, the main reason for the translation of the ever strengthening movement for putting Scottish affairs under con-trol of the people in Scotland from the field of national sentiment into that of pressing economic necessity.

In the meantime, the genius of the Scottish nation is still as lively as ever. Head for head, twice as many Scots go right through the Universities, as students in England. And it may be that one of these young Scots may have touched off a train of events as invigorating as that released by young Matthew Dobson two centuries ago. In the summer of 1894, the then youthful Charles Wilson marvelled at the coloured glory of the heavens as he saw it from the top of Ben Nevis. That vision led him directly to con-trive the unique 'cloud chamber' that, more than any other single piece of apparatus, unlocked the inner secrets of the atom.

If atomic power ever comes to anything, as seems very likely, it will be, so far as Great Britain is concerned, most conveniently released in mass among the hills and mountains of Scotland. That's for the reason that it is only there that water enough can be found, and high reservoirs built, to allow the reactors to function evenly through the day and all through the night. As may be done in Wales, but never in England, they are already building what is called a 'pumped storage' scheme on the shoulder of Cruachan in Lochaber. It will store and release power lined up all the way from Hunterston on the Firth of Clyde.

CHAPTER NINE

THE LETTERS OF SCOTLAND

'LET me make the songs of a country, and I care not who makes its laws,' said a passing wise man. But a true nation always sings and dances to the spring of its own fiddle.

In all the Western world, including the fair land of England, there is no richer store of songs and ballads than in Scotland. Their words rose from the soil and their music was carried on the breeze. Among the mountains and in the islands, the sun follows the rain, the colours are forever changing and the procession of human life is revealed in stark tones of light and shade. There the songs are mostly wild and sad. In the softer regions, where the daily round is less in the presence of the almighty, they are couthy and merry.

But the songs of the Highlands and Lowlands alike all grew to that same music which is both the mother and the daughter of poetry. Their cadence and measure followed that same broken five note scale which was sung by the Egyptians in the building of their temples, and by the Greeks returning from Marathon. There is something magic about this pentatonic notation. It may be that it comforts the tongue over the natural break in the register of the ordinary human voice. It certainly sounds easier to the untutored human ear than any exactly balanced temperamental scale can ever do. Still alive in the East, the pentatonic scale is now limited, as a living thing in the West, to the fringes of Europe. Recently, odd composers of instrumental music have sought to capture its mystery by striking only the black keys on the piano. But only the artless human voice can do it justice. English people may get the taste of it from the 'flamenco' music of Andalusia, or, in their own tongue, from a good rendering of the ballad *Barbara Allan*. That goes to an air out of Lewis in the Hebrides that Samuel Pepys first heard from his 'little Scotch maid'. But

the real blas (taste) is only to be savoured as the singing men bend
to the oars off the islands of the Western sea, or the women sing
and rock to the waulking (stretching) of the cloth.

It was very largely this ancient, simple music that preserved
the poetry of Scotland, and with it the letters of the country, when
all the outward forces seemed set to destroy them. Much more
than the pedants of to-day are aware, Scottish writing, in straight
English and in Scots, is indebted to the bard who gave tongue to
the deeds of the Celtic warriors so long ago. All the better to
remember their trials on the field of battle, and their essays in
the lists of love, he put his words into poetry and then to song.
(One will note the sung jingles in the advertising inserts on television.) As times changed, the bard fell from that high estate when
he might win a strong house, a herd of fine cattle, or a good sword,
for a tale, a snatch of verse, or a song.

His spoken art, though still heard in remote places where tellers
of tales enliven the long winter evenings without benefit of print,
became but a remnant. But as the printed page could not sound
aloud, his singing voice remained robustly alive. As more time
passed, the airs on the wind came to the ears of Robert Burns.
The lyrical words which he strung to them were thus remembered as they were heard. It was the matchless songs of Burns
that gave renewed honour to the old Scottish tongue and stayed
its decay. Walter Scott, for his part, embroidered the stories that
were culled from the countryside by such as Joseph Train, the
travelling gauger (excise-man) from Sorn. With them, he knotted
together the broken threads in Scottish prose. Right enough, both
Robert Burns and Walter Scott owed as much to their native land
as it to them.

They were able to draw from the treasuries of music and of
storied lore that the bards had plenished. To grasp how they were
placed to do this, one must be on intimate terms with the country
and familiar with the loom of language. In particular, the songs,
ballads, poems, stories and mouth music generally of Scotland
have been fashioned out of the native stuffs of the country on the
frame of language. (The term 'mouth music' is also used in a
narrower sense to describe a rapidly sung accompaniment to
dancing.) The strong warp in the broad Scots tongue is mainly
of Saxon origin. But the woof or web which adds the colour and
makes the pattern is, for the most part, the gift of these Celts who,

at the same time, have kept their own language. The texture comes from the general country and the finish is bright from washing in the mountain streams and airing on the hills.

Right enough, to lay hold of what the present offers and the future portends for the spoken, sung and written word in Scotland, as indeed for the other arts, one must have a firm grip of the past. Centuries after the ancient Gaelic tongue was edged into slow retreat to the mountains and islands by the Saxon Queen Margaret and her half-Saxon son, King David, it none the less remained the paramount tongue over most of Scotland. It was strongly sustained by ready communion with Ireland. Indeed the Celtic scholars of the two countries used the same written language until the main bodies of their people diverged in religious faith. An additional barrier was then put between them by the plantation of Ulster by Covenanting and thus very Protestant Scots.

Now, in spite of what Dr. Samuel Johnson, who knew so much and again so little, recounted after his tour of the Hebrides in 1773, the old tongue quite readily carried the book learning of the times. Apart from the Ossianic tales of the bards, the miracles and religious commentaries, and the involved treatises on the making of poetry, it was quite adequate for the medicine and science of the age. Some of the text books of the physicians, like the MacLeans of Skye or the Beatons of Mull, were quite innocent of English. In one of these medical works, the colouring of the human face in illness is described with a surprisingly modern touch. Then, though the Gaelic-speaking area contracted, and with it the proportion of the nation using that language, the absolute number of those with Gaelic as a mother tongue steadily increased until well into the nineteenth century.

In figures, the half of the Scottish nation who spoke Gaelic habitually in the sixteenth century ran to about 150,000 people. But the diminished one-fifth who still held by it in 1800 mustered around 325,000 souls. Right until the Industrial Revolution, the Gaelic tongue, which marched with Scots over a very wide front was therefore, albeit hard pressed, far from being the beleaguered speech that it is to-day. Though now weak in the newly printed word, it was still strong in the mouths of the people, all the more since the old tongue is by nature a singing language.

In the long meantime, the Saxon language from Northumbria

had been powerfully advertised by the kingly succession over the low lying and more benign parts of Scotland.

For a long time this speech ranged over the Border and far down into England without any marked break. Thomas the Rhymer, who 'spied a ferlie wi' his ee', John Barbour who sang of the Bruce, Henry the Minstrel who struck his harp to Wallace, and Andrew Wyntoun who lamented the passing of plenty of 'ale and brede, wyne and wax, gamyn and gle' with the good King Alexander, were as easily understood in York as in Edinburgh or Aberdeen. James the First who penned the *King's Quair* was on familiar literary terms with Geoffrey Chaucer and John Gower, the poets of England. It is indeed from that old heritage that the Scottish schoolboy of to-day, especially in the country parts, has the edge over his English fellow in coming to familiarity with the *Canterbury Tales*. The same sounds are still in his head.

However, with the Wars of Independence and the stabilisation of the frontier, the ordinary tongue of England drew away from the 'Inglis' speech of Scotland. While the language of the southern kingdom took to another mode, the 'Inglis' of Scotland actually held closer to the original Saxon. Shortly it was so differentiated as to become known as 'Scottis'. Even in this present age of fixing print, one sees the same moving apart of 'American'.

During the years of the Auld Alliance with France, this now separated speech obtained a large infusion from the French. This came more by way of vocabulary than by construction and idiom as previously in England. To this day the Scottish housewife puts her 'gigot' (leg of mutton) in an 'ashet' (earthenware dish), salts it from a 'crock' (large jar) and in less polite society, throws her slops in a 'jaw box' (sink).

If this latter word has done good service to the 'Scotch comics' it has also puzzled the learned philologists. But one fancies that it is simply 'jaup box', the 'jaup' being the Scots for 'splash' and the 'box' being the French *boite*, as in the English 'boot' of a motor car. Indeed, as the Scottish byreman comes nearer to Chaucerian English than the Oxford don of to-day, his milch cow, which comes to '*s'aproche*' or '*prochy*' has a lot more French than the average day tripper out of London. Students with a mind to deeper enquiry may discover a rich mine of French in Scottish architecture. The outside or 'scalestair', once common in Scottish tenements, is none other than *escalier*.

During this period of intimate traffic with the Continent, through France, Latin also became a vogue among the literati. And, Scottish schooling being what it was, odd tags penetrated into the common vernacular. To this day, the Glasgow women-folk use 'impertinent' in the sense of 'cheeky' without knowing that the word was first flung at some scholar who was not to the point. And the Aberdeenshire farm servant may oddly say 'he's on his potestator'. It was during this period of estrangement with England and close communion with the Continent that the Scottish 'makars' of poetry and song were at work. Over the years when the poets of England, between the times of Geoffrey Chaucer and Edmund Spenser, were muted, Scotland was filled with very masculine writers and singers.

The great company included such as Patrick Johnstoun, Robert Henryson, William Dunbar, Quintine Shaw, Gavin Douglas, David Lindsay and James the Fifth. Very significantly, the Stewarts were already a writing race when the English monarchs remained rough men, and indeed the most of them ruffians, of the armed camp. Up until the time of James the Sixth, who also had a writing itch, they gave a royal cachet to what became known as 'Court Scots'. That latter king actually wrote the 'Reulis and Cautelis to be Observit and Eschewit in Scottish Poesie' before he migrated over the Border to polish up his English. This polite-ness has never really gone from Scots, so that to-day what is known as 'Broad Scots' has a social standing beyond the compass of any rustic speech in England.

After the 'makars', writing in Scots took a great tumble, at the very time when the more feminine Elizabethans of England were about to come into their own. Nor need there be any great mystery about this. As the English scene settled, that in Scotland became turbulent with religious struggle. But the great blow was dealt by the advent of printing and of the Bible in English. The two basic-ally Saxon languages tended to come together in the written and printed word. Out of this, the polite speech of the country was put under increasing pressure of change. Though one fancies that his accents would still smack very much of his native land, John Knox himself was faulted for 'knappin' sudron'—essaying the English style.

There was also the fact that, out of the intimate commerce of Scotland with the Continent, more of the deep scholarship and of the general letters of the country had come to be carried in Latin than in neighbouring England. Though brought up to Gaelic and Scots, the European fame of George Buchanan as a poet and playwright is now lost in that ancient language. William Dunbar's *Lament for the Makars*, in which he recalled his departed Scots writing brethren to the recurring theme of *timor mortis conturbat me* (the fear of death disquiets me), became almost a tract for the times. Out of the four languages over which Scottish literature was spread at the time of the Reformation, namely Scots, English, Gaelic and Latin, it soon looked, when Latin was increasingly locked up in the study, as if English were going to carry off the palm.

However the Scots tongue which had come in through the front door and up the main staircase, even to the chamber of the king, did not slink down the backstair and out by the back door, as did the regional speeches in England. Though as bad as expelled from the new printeries it remained not only the language of the common folk in the Lowlands, but also, from its 'lang pedigree' that of the law courts, the counting houses and even of some of the castles. And in the Highlands and Islands, Gaelic though now rarely committed to writing, far less to print, remained on the lips of the people. Seeping in at the grass roots, as it were, this old tongue had by this time given more than a tinge to Scots.

Touching on this, there are those in the literary coteries in Scotland to-day who make out that Gaelic has had little or no influence on the Scots which they sometimes affect in their writings. Their scholarship is as lame as was that of Sir Walter Scott when he averred that the Celtic and Gothic languages, being 'radically different and totally distinct', were incapable of amalgamating, and thus without influence on one another. Now it is true enough that the Gaelic and Teutonic tongues (like English or Scots) are quite different in construction, grammar and philosophy. Mutual borrowings are thus apt to be heavily disguised. For example the publicity men of Hollywood and Pinewood are hardly likely to recognise 'slogan' (cry of the people), 'whisky' (water of life), 'glamour' (a witch's spell) and now 'oomph', as coming from the Gaelic.

As for 'blackmail', it is in fact none other than the *maille dubh*, the under cover or 'black' tribute levied by the Highland caterans on those who had more money but less skill with the sword. Nor are they likely to know that 'shoot, it's smashing' is near enough the phonetic ring of the Gaelic for 'go ahead, it's good'. As anyone with the necessary equipment may well discover from the works of Robert Burns, Gaelic has contributed a very great deal to the stock of words in Scots. It has also given a turn of phrasing like the definites in 'I have the cold the day', and a twist in pronunciation, as in 'Loch Lomond'. To add to that, it has given a ring, a lilt and a metre to the once Saxon tongue which traversed the Border. This latter, as will presently be shown, was of very great consequence in the revival of Scots.

To run the years together, since this work seeks the formative causes of the continuing Scottishness of Scotland, rather than aims to be a chronological history, the life ebbed out of letters in Scots and Gaelic for almost two centuries after the Court took the road to England. The literary men who thronged into Edinburgh to gild its 'Golden Age' as the eighteenth century wore on all sought a precise diction in written English. To match the new Italian hand, and to gain a market, stiff and grand writing was all the mode. David Hume submitted his works to a fisher-out of Scotticisms. Class lessons were given, and taken, in the removal of northern 'barbarisms'.

But the spoken accents in the coffee and wine shops, among the Crochallan Fencibles for example, and in familiar moments at home, were anything but redolent of London society. James Boswell was really something of a comical oddity in his efforts to get rid of uttered Scotticisms. His father, the old Lord Auchinkeck who said of Samuel Johnson that 'he keepit a schule, but ca'd it an academy', and his son, Sir Alexander Boswell, who wrote *Jenny's Bawbee*, were much more in the true Scottish character. Though the philosophy of David Hume, the political economy of Adam Smith and the history of William Robertson were all, with an eye to the market in the south, in the straightest possible English, they were discussed in broad enough Scots.

As for the singers and poets, they found that short of giving themselves over entirely to the English muse, like James Thomson with his *Seasons*, which meant, for full success, removing to England in the time of their grandfathers (a juggling with time that was manifestly out of the question) they might as well stick to the themes of their native land. Now the church, which had been a butt and betimes a bield to the earlier 'makars' was now cast in too stern a mould either to enrage or harbour them. The king and the politicians, with most of the free cash, were in London. There was nothing for it but to strike again the native harp to lays that appealed to the people around them. These folk, if now used to print in English, heard with a Scottish ear.

Casting around for an instrument, the Lowland poets found it ready made and newly shone in the Highlands. Over the hills, where verse and song passed from mouth to mouth, the press, which thrived on printed English had found no provender. There, on the bare but still healthy pasturage, the genius of Gaelic had come to life again. In new bardic measures, Mary, the daughter of Red Alasdair, and Duncan Ban MacIntyre, Fair Duncan the joiner's son, with many more, both men and women, were singing and telling stories in praise of *tir nam beann, nan gleann, nan gaisgach* (the land of the bens, the glens, and the heroes). James MacPherson brought the taste of their work to English by translating in a grand manner the epic Gaelic poetry of Ossian.

It is little to the present purpose whether, as is still in argument, he found and Englished the old forgotten Celtic poems, or simply made them up. His works became best-sellers to the point of being beside the pillow of Napoleon Bonaparte. Who knows, the volume may have been a minding from that Marshal MacDonald, Duke of Taranto, and victor at Wagram, who learned Gaelic from his father, the same Neil MacDonald of Clanranald in the Uists who guided Flora MacDonald and Betty Burke (Prince Charles Edward Stewart) to the waiting ship, and went with him to France. The old Gaelic embattled behind the mountains and the English which might be framed to it was given a new glory. At the same time, the two Highland risings and the succeeding bitter repression by Butcher Cumberland had given a stir to patriotic feeling all over Scotland.

In Edinburgh, Allan Ramsay, looking to the singing hills, and again to the threatening south, was moved to return to that other tongue of Scotland, the Scots which he had brought from his native Leadhills, in the heart of the Lowlands. Now the Gaels, from the virtue of their language, had never taken to rhyming the end syllables at the end of verse lines. Their poetry hung on the marrying of the sounds and the swing of words. Being, like the blank verse of Shakespeare, for declamation and singing, and not for the eye, it rang naturally to the old bardic five note scale. The pure airs which it preserved and constantly renewed were carried over all Scotland, and to airts (directions) where all memory of Gaelic as a spoken tongue had long since gone.

To this day, the very broad doric 'bothy ballads' of Aberdeen-shire mostly go to tunes that were first intoned by the Gaels. It was only natural, from the sounds around him, that the new measures in Scots which Ramsay put into his *Gentle Shepherd* and *Tea Table Miscellany* should breathe something of the old Gaelic airs. The same went for Robert Ferguson when he took up the same declamatory and singing harp and in turn passed it on to Robert Burns.

Now, Robert Burns was more than a poet of unsurpassed genius. He was, as some poets certainly are not, a very remarkable man. Embodying all the virtues and most of the vices of the two main blood streams in the Scottish race, he projected the many sided image of Scotland.

But Robert Burns would never have appeared to the common view as the 'everyman' that he was, save that he was born and brought to manhood in Scotland, and nowhere else. In England his genius, perchance, might have budded. But it could never have opened up in full flower in that country. It took the birth-right gifts of the two races of Scotland to compound the brilliant treasure which was his portion, and which he passed on to Scot-land and to the world.

The Presbyterian Kirk, whose counsels of virtue were some-times put to him far too obviously to be followed, placed him in the way of an education which would have been far beyond his ploughman's station in neighbouring England. That was the main contribution of the Lowlands.

To his further great good fortune, the presentation of the High-lands was a great body of ready made and very choice tunes and melodies. These were rarer and more delicate than those that carried the rough Border ballads. The first fame of Robert Burns rested on putting matchless lyrical words in the Scots tongue to the old lilting music which constantly sounded down from the mountains of the singing Gaelic bards. Incidentally, the so called 'Burnsian stanza', which he drew from Robert Ferguson and de-veloped, exactly suits the old broken scale of the Gaels. It may also be said that since his time many of the melodies have been as bad as murdered by the keyed piano.

In the meantime the Scots, who came late to printing (the first press was set up in Edinburgh in 1508, and others were set going at St. Andrews in 1552, and at Stirling in 1560) had been very fruitfully active with the mechanics of literature. By 1790, the dozen or so paper mills around Edinburgh were sending fine paper as far away as London. On the printing side, William Ged invented stereotyping in Edinburgh. In Glasgow, the brothers Robert and Andrew Foulis achieved such a perfection in type faces and in letterpress as to be called the 'Elzeviers of Scotland', after the famous Dutch printers of that name. In the matter of publishing, a group in Edinburgh, rightly conceiving that there might be a market for well marshalled and indexed learning started what is now the *Encyclopaedia Britannica*.

As the nineteenth century opened, both Edinburgh and Glasgow filled up with printeries and publishing houses. Especially in Edinburgh, where magazines proliferated, reviewing became a veritable local industry. The whole region smelled of printers' ink. Apart from business acumen, the one main reason for that was that, as a bounty of Presbyterian piety, the generality could read and write, when substantial books were still a 'class' preserve in more benighted England. And, as a by product, intelligent and literate labour could be had for the printing works. These workmen too would be all the more painstaking since, apart from the slender works of the poets, practically all the copy they set in print and read in proof, would sound foreign if read out loud, however familiar it might have become to the eye.

Getting back to the actual writers, Walter Scott put Scots back into narrative prose with his tales and dialogue. Like Robert Burns, he owed everything to his native land. As already indicated, his minstrelsy and prose were embellished by the stories in the Scots tongue brought to him from the countryside. Scott pulled aside the veil which, though passable to song, still obscured the colour, romance and manliness of the Highlands. Indeed, when the Gaels and their language were now going through a time of great stress he over-romanticised their land and their ways. From Scott's time on, as with the poets after Burns, prose writers in Scotland became less self conscious of the English of England.

Typified by Robert Louis Stevenson, they began to flavour that language with a native essence, as the North Americans are now doing. It was no longer a case of going over literary works with a fine toothcomb for imbedded Scotticisms. Certainly, some of the 'Kailyairders', those who spaded the kitchen garden, hard by the village pump, tended to go to the other extreme. They pictured Scotland as a sort of stagey rustic retreat, with all the props showing. None the less, from their whistle-binkies (seats beside the organ pipes) these very worthy people turned over the store of Scots words and aired the idiom. Apart from the inserts and these very earthy works, Scots was left to the poets, songsters and balladiers.

Yet the old language was still in the mouths of the people, and it still held on to its social status. It was a lady of high degree, Lady Nairne, who penned such enduring favourites as *The Land o' the Leal*, *The Laird o' Cockpen* and the stirring *A Hundred Pipers* . . . Nor was she alone at the task in my lady's chamber.

Since then, there has been a continual flow of verse in Scots. National occasions, like the reiving (lifting) of the Stone of Destiny have been marked by real spates. Much of the work is of course no more than doggerel. Nevertheless it indicates a deep down feeling which will not be denied.

In this past generation there has been a strong revival in the use of Scots for poetry, other than lyrics, ballads and light verse. This however has never yet caught the common eye and ear, in anything like the same measure as the works of the 'Kailyairders'. To be sure, much of the new work is far too visibly contrived in what is called 'Plastic Scots' to look and sound like the real thing from the countryside and town vennels that was the stuff of Robert Burns. Its practitioners are perhaps too consciously 'non folksy'. Yet Hugh MacDiarmid (Christopher Murray Grieve) and those others who have modelled Scots themselves, define a powerful trend. Sooner or later, some one among them will discover the secret, as Robert Burns did, of a tried and tested vehicle.

For its part, the old Gaelic tongue, which for long years resisted the destructive printing press with more success than Scots and which through its natural music provided the reviving elixir for that speech, is now greatly diminished in new writing. Yet, with no distinction between the language of the poets and the prose scholars, its literature remains much more of a unity. And its new poets like Somhairle MacLean and Derick Thomson have been more successful in catching the spirit and mood of the ebbing band of native Gaelic speakers, than their Scots writing brethren.

The big thing to-day is that both Scots and Gaelic are now penetrating deeply into ordinary Scottish speech and general literature, as a leaven of idiom, construction and vocabulary. A leader writer in a sober Scottish newspaper may now use such words as 'thole' (put up with) or 'darg' (day's work) without resorting to inverted commas. And the command of a few words in Gaelic, like *slainte mhath* (good health) or *beannaich leibh* (blessings on you) has become very fashionable. There is also this advantage that those who want to be as Englished as, say, James Boswell generally take leave of the country, or acquire such a turn of speech that they hardly pass for Scots. Bearing on this, it may be said that for centuries a departure from bed and board does not alone constitute desertion in Scotland. Living apart within the very same house is alike a ground for divorce.

CHAPTER TEN

SCOTTISH ARTS AND LIFE

'*Macbeth.* Go bid thy mistress, when my drink is ready, she strike upon the bell. Get thee to bed. (*Exit servant.*) Is this a dagger that I see before me, the handle toward my hand. Come, let me clutch thee. . . .'

When William Shakespeare took very considerable dramatic licence in making out the Mormaer MacBeth to be as murderous a villain as that Richard the Third of England who had the little princes done to death in the Tower, London boasted at least five public theatres and several private establishments.

True enough, those early theatres, like the famous Globe, gave cover only to the actors and to a select, highly placed few among the audience, and by a thatched roof at that. For the rest, those who paid their money had to stand in the open yard or 'pit'. But London was then a largish city crowded with monied people at a loose end. It could also depend on long spells of reasonable weather. In short, Shakespeare was able to muster that requisite for every successfully working dramatist, a good paying house. If 'rare' Ben Jonson had been fated to be reared in the Annandale in Scotland of his father, he would never have been able, for the lack of it, to run Shakespeare a close race.

Right enough, it needs more than a fount of genius and talent to well up the arts. The Scots were well abreast of the English in staging the old 'miracle and morality' plays in churches and market places. But they lagged behind when it came to professionally written, acted and platform mounted drama. David Lindsay's remarkable *Thrie Estaitis* was actually produced before the Court and in the open air at the Playfield in Edinburgh in 1554, some years before the first emergence of English comedy and tragedy, properly so called. But there was practically nothing in the way of a recognisable Scottish theatre until Edinburgh eventually came to house a sufficient public with a little money to burn. The literati were then entertained by Allan Ramsay's *Gentle Shepherd* and later by John Home's *Douglas*. Robert Burns, of course, also had a go at writing for the stage, though in another vein, with his tuneful cantata *The Jolly Beggars*.

Though Home was himself a minister, it has long been the fashion, in certain quarters, to fault the Presbyterian Kirk for this slow growth of the theatre in Scotland. That accusation has been faithfully copied from one speech and piece of writing to another, just like the groundless complaint, in face of the facts of the wars with England, that it 'dinged doon' all the abbeys. Certainly the grave Kirk (which actually has its own theatre in the 'Gateway' in Edinburgh to-day) did not favour worldly works of no substance. But over the whole range of the arts, from architecture and working in silver to painting in oils, it released infinitely more genius than, at the very worst count, it ever suppressed.

One fancies that the weather, combined with the scarcity of strong, long timber had as much to do with the slow growth of the Scottish theatre as anything else. While a roofless theatre might do the turn in London, it just did not serve in Edinburgh. Until quite late in the day, it just was not possible in Scotland to roof over widely spaced walls for places of common assembly. It was all very well for Dr. Samuel Johnson to crack : 'A tree might be a show in Scotland, as a horse in Venice', or to joke : 'Consider, sir, the value of such a piece of timber here', when he lost his walking stick in Mull. Over most of England there was plenty of good building wood. Hence those picturesque full and half timbered houses in those parts of that country where building stone was hard to come by.

In Scotland, on the other hand, the shortage of long baulks of wood was at the root of many things that are distinctively Scottish. One might mention the turret-carrying corbels of stepped out stone that are a feature of Scottish baronial architecture, the old kirks as narrow as coffins, and the pack-of-card house frontages in the old town of Edinburgh. In the still older days, the royal court and the prelatic church had been able to make away with the best of the common store of timber. But remembering also that large pieces could not be imported on any scale and that many of the convenient forests had been put to the flames in the recurrent invasions from England, with their going the available common stock came to be shared more equitably.

One can see that visually in the way Scottish domestic architecture drew together to a common pattern after the Reformation. The great lordly castles gave way to extremely functional timber saving fortalices. At the same time, the houses of the town merchants, while not needing the same thick protective walls, approximated upwards to the same sort of corbelled and turreted style. The levelling out is demonstrated in the little town of Culross across the Firth of Forth from Edinburgh. Like the walls of York, the towers of Carcasonne in France or the raised footways in Chester, Culross is eloquent in its stones. One may, of course, make too much of single factors in this functional shaping. All sorts of factors conspire together to make a general pattern. It is interesting to reflect that both the draped four poster bed and the thick padded raiment that are so typical of Elizabethan England are ascribed to the low indoor temperatures which, out of the then lack of good firing, had to be suffered. And, in turn, the furniture of Chippendale, Hepplewhite and Sheraton owed as much to the importation of new woods, and to the perfection of steel that could take a good cutting edge, as to genius in design.

However, to get back to communal entertainment, what the Scots lost on the swings they gained on the roundabouts. With the need to huddle together to share out creature comfort from the available resources of fuel, the minstrel in the hall and the story teller in the buttery lingered far longer in Scotland than in England.

That had a great deal to do with the accumulation and preservation of the Scottish wealth in balladry and in simple singing measures. As times changed, the house gathering, variously known as the 'lift' in Scots, or as the *ceilidh'* (caley) in Gaelic, came to be something very native that the English can never match. With its singing and stories and acting the part, this informal meeting nurtured the qualities of drama which suddenly burst out more openly in the community drama movements which swept Scotland in the 1920's.

But to be sure, the Scots made no great impact on stagecraft, properly speaking, until James Matthew Barrie very successfully marketed in London the whimsicalities which he brought out of his native Kirriemuir and deftly touched up on his journey. To the good of his purse and the store of his medals, Barrie was certainly a master of framing and spinning out a simple plot. As such, he is amply due a kindly memory. But his 'little people' being born out of fragments of 'baby laughter' are nothing like the ferlies that beckoned True Thomas to elf-land or like the 'wee green folk' that, as some say, disport nightly in the Highlands to this day. The late James Bridie (O. H. Mavor), a Glasgow medical man turned playwright, though a man of great parts was also somewhat short in touching the essential Scottish scene. None the less, he greatly encouraged the new corps of native writers for the stage that has recently gathered in the country.

Linking themselves with the renaissance in Scottish letters, these new playwrights have made a promising return to Scots. And the last few years have witnessed what never was before, namely the first signs of drama in Scottish Gaelic. The difficulty is that by its very Scottishness, a play in Scots, and certainly in Gaelic, is ruled out of the really profitable rounds in the south. There is thus the problem of making it pay. However, the new writers have stuck to it with native resolution and they have drawn a certain sustenance from the very strong amateur movement which exists and thrives in the country. Just to show how a land change makes all the difference to drama, as to everything else, some of the best new work in the Scottish theatre has been in the field of historical drama.

That is to say, just as the English are modernising Shakespeare, some of the leading Scottish playwrights have harked back to the costume and speech of centuries ago. That has not been, as many might suppose, out of nostalgia for the lost past. Like the movement of the English in the exactly opposite direction, it is in aid of greater acceptance. The point is that there is now no general standard, like 'stage English' for speaking in Scots. The actors and even more so the actresses therefore tend to strike it at different levels and with very varying regional accents. Above the level of very local kitchen stuff, the resultant mixture therefore tends to be very uneven in texture. Hence the resort to the common denominator of 'Court Scots', as in Robert MacLellan's *Jamie the Saxt* or Alexander Reid's *Toom Byres* (empty cowhouses).

The native Scottish theatre, apart from writing for the straight English market, has never yet won the position enjoyed by Dublin drama in its best days. But it is now represented on the boards by more than the 'Scotch comic' as he was typed by the incomparable Harry Lauder. It should be said that this comic, when at his best, is by no means a slight character. He combines a grave respectability, even in drink, with stout independence and rich, pawky humour. His art, even when Englished, cannot readily be translated over the Border.

Surprisingly enough, though it may seem to those many, within and without the country, who have never taken the trouble to look up and consider the relevant dates and facts, and who imagine the contrary, the Reformation greatly fostered the arts in Scotland. It brought on especially those that are native to the land. Nor need there be any wonder at that. If the religious upheaval stilled the emotions, by banishing supernatural fears, it opened up the schools and the intellect. In the person of George Jameson of Aberdeen (1588-1644), Scotland boasted a considerable native painter years before England had even got to the point of hiring foreign limners, like Holbein, Rubens, Van Dyck and many more.

Considering that England was much richer, ten times more populous and had never broken up the frame of the Roman Church, the emergence of Jameson was significant. Nor was it less telling that, in later years, Presbyterian Glasgow came to house the first recognisable regional school of painting in Britain.

The Scots always had a flair for design and colour. That may be seen from the old Pictish and Celtic carvings, the painted boards in the early churches, and the Border and Harris tweeds of to-day. But the country was in no position to make any great show during the long years of wasting war with England; more so since the Roman church either imported craftsmen or bought most of its furnishing ready-made from abroad. Against that, the Scots were always in closer traffic with the Continent, so that the standards were maintained and refreshed.

After Jameson, his followers, John Scougal and David Paton, began to fill the country with portraits, both life size and in miniature. In passing it should perhaps be said in defence of the line of Scottish artists that the fabulous, in more senses than one, likenesses of the unbroken line of one hundred and ten Scottish kings in the gallery of Holyrood Palace are from the brush of an incomer. That was an industrious Fleming, named De Wett, who turned out his goods, as it were, on a production belt. But easel painting did not become a substantial thing until canvasses, oil pigments and customers became more freely available after the Union of the Parliaments in 1707. As the eighteenth century moved on, Edinburgh came to house a busy and successful school of painters.

Giving credit where credit is due, oddly enough that got a start from the cash that was trundled up from the south in wagons to give the Scots a float for taking over a good part of the exclusively English National Debt. Some small part of the new money put into circulation went to the founding of the 'School of St. Luke' in Edinburgh. It was fortunate in having notable artists at its head, and eventually it threw up Allan Ramsay, the son of the poet of the same name, as a fashionable portraitist. He in turn gave rise to a regular galaxy whose brightest star was Henry Raeburn. Thanks partly to the whisky advertisers, his Highland chieftains are especially well known to-day.

In the meantime, as the design school of St. Luke faded away, things began to pick up rapidly in Glasgow. Reflecting this, the brothers Foulis, the same who won great fame as fine printers, set up a school of art in that city in 1753. Out of that, the Glasgow Academy of the Fine Arts was set going in 1759, nine years before the Royal Academy was founded in London. This pioneer academy, which absorbed all too much of the time and money of the Foulis's, collapsed in 1775. But it left a lasting memorial in the public exhibition of art, the first of these in Britain being held in the quadrangle of Glasgow University. And it provided a new series of able heads for the new school of design which was established in Edinburgh in 1760.

It was this new school that set a very Scottish seal on the native art. Glasgow trained Alexander Runciman struck out into subject pictures. He was followed by David Wilkie, the reputed father of landscape painting in Scotland. It was the Board of Manufacturers, financed with hush-money from England, that finally managed to put a little system into the affairs of the Scottish artists. In Scotland, as everywhere else, these individualists could not hang together. In 1819 their Institution for the Encouragement of the Fine Arts was built up on the loose bones of the former Society of Incorporated Artists. But it took the prosaic Board of Manufacturers to give them a home in the Royal Institution which it opened on the Mound in Edinburgh in 1826. At length

the separateness of Scottish art was acknowledged by the charter-
ing of the Royal Scottish Academy in 1837.

One cannot of course go into all the ins and outs of painting
in Scotland, nor mention all the names. The present intent is
rather to seek out root formative causes. It must suffice to say
that with the emergence of Glasgow as the dominant commercial
and industrial centre in Scotland, the productive artists moved
to that city. There, in a few brief years, and as no other single city
in Britain has ever witnessed, they worked up that Glasgow
School of Painting which commanded the homage of Europe.
There were many reasons for this native and very brilliant flower-
ing. But they all came back to the same old causative things.
These were the free democratic communion of the city, the lettered independence of the Presbyterian Kirk, and the coal and
ironstone which put the merchants and industrialists in the way
to afford generous patronage.

Bearing on patronage, there was also the very important point
that the city of Glasgow had long set aside odd sums of money
for the 'Common Good'. Out of this fund and by munificent
donations and legacies the city itself provided an encouraging
ambiente by gathering a general art collection which has no peer
in Britain to-day. Then there were the flaming colours of the sky
in the west, the violently contrasting tones and hues of the crowded
city and of the empty wild at its very gates. Additionally, the Scots,
out of their history, were at ease in their wanderings so that they
could freely borrow from the Italians, Dutch, Spanish and French
without denying their own land. In advance of the French, the
Scots, thanks to all this, broke with tradition and gave their works
a strong stamp of Scottish impressionistic realism. It only needs
the revival of the city's business in a free Scotland to bring a
Glasgow School of Painting together again.

Going on to the other arts, the Scots always had a good eye and
hand for shape and form. That is seen alike in the curious twined
patterns of the distant Pictish past (the animal and human form
was abjured), in the metal work in the Hunterston brooch of
Celtic times, and in the fantastic carvings, like something out of
Angkor, in the Roslin Kirk, just outside Edinburgh. But for long
they could not go beyond the tools, materials and means available
in the country.

Far from being set back by the Reformation artcraft, working in wood never became much of a thing in Scotland until the religious times were settled. That same settling released a great store of pent up native talent in the working of precious metals, especially silver. In this field the essential dichogamy and dichotomy of Scotland asserted itself. In the Lowlands, the ornate sacerdotal vessels of the past, which had mostly been imported, gave way to native-made communion cups of puritan plainness but of great beauty. Showing how one thing impinges on another, these cups were rather more generous in capacity than in former times. That came about because the sacrament was no longer a priestly mystery, but was dispensed to the laity, who liked a hearty draught.

In the Highlands, on the other hand, beauty in silver ware was sought and attained in surpassing gaiety. The silver mounted and inlaid dirks, broadswords, pistols and powder horns of the Highlanders became things of matchless perfection. Delicately worked and chased silver was lavished on the great war-pipes and on the buckles and brooches of the Highland dress. The two divergent schools of silver smithing then came together in copying in metal the shallow quaichs, with lugged handles, that had come down in staved or carved wood from the distant past. To this day, the retiring President of the Bowling Club receives, as likely as not, a silver quaich embodying the art skill of both the Highlands and the Lowlands.

The same inexorable influences can be readily discerned in Scottish architecture. In a society where delusions of grandeur were held in check and at length defeated by the natural land, neither the monarch, the barons nor the prelates had ever been able to build in that magnificence which marked their state in England. The Reformation of religion, with its spread of learning, political power and social democracy, brought about a further levelling. The least part of it was that the 'whigmaleeries, curliewurlies and opensteek hems' which raised the ire of Andrew Fairservice in Walter Scott's *Rob Roy* were banished out of new churches. On this point it may as well be said that neither John Calvin nor John Knox were enemies of beauty in form and colour.

In his *Institutes* Calvin counselled : 'For as much as carving and painting are the gifts of God, I require that they be both pure and lawfully used.' And at the present time of writing, the Kirk of Scotland has just sent a minding round the Presbyteries and

Kirk Sessions suggesting that unless the stained glass offered to
the churches be worthy, the windows had best be left plain, to let
in the pure unsullied light of heaven. One may agree that there
have been times when the Anglican chapters could have done with
such advice.

While still different in size and accommodation, the houses of
the country people, the city merchants, the craftsmen and the
rural gentry all began to approximate in style.

No stone or piece of timber was put in place if it did not serve
an immediate function. This economy in building materials was
furthered by the need to squeeze together and thus save on room
firing. That 'a blast o' Janwar win' blew hansel in on Robin' in
a kitchen partitioned from the cattle within the same walls in the
'auld clay biggin' in Alloway, did not mean that the family of
Robert Burns was ground down to the uttermost. The cows, with
the 'hole in the wall' bed were part of the domestic heating
arrangements. After all, there was a time, even in England, when
such a well paid functionary as Samuel Pepys could furnish no
better sleeping quarters for his maidservant than under his dining
table.

This extreme functionalism, which came to be softened by
decorative ideas out of France and the Netherlands can still be
studied in the old town of Edinburgh or in the little fisher towns
that line the Fife coast. And an interesting application lingers in
the 'chalmer end' of the Moray coast. There, parents commonly
add a room at the end of their own house for a newly married
daughter. As times change, they then move into the same
chamber, while the daughter and her growing family, flit into the
main house. Out of this organic way of living, it was no uncom-
mon thing for a Lord of Session to live in the top storey of an
Edinburgh tenement while his 'caddy' bedded down on the
ground floor, nearer the smells of the street.

With the growth of trade and the coming of more worldly prosperous times, the Scots, as may be seen by the stately buildings
and ample squares of the New Town of Edinburgh, made a great
jump into classicism. The towns in the fast developing industrial
belt were re-modelled and filled with churches and public buildings like Greek temples. If the Scots in the past had been handi-
capped by having too little means, this time they suffered from
having too much, and too quickly acquired. Finally, after a trend

back to mock 'Scottish baronial' in the larger buildings, like the Abbotsford mansion of Walter Scott, or the Balmoral Castle of the royal family, Charles Rennie Mackintosh at length fused the traditional native style with the last word in modernity.

Certainly, as commonly happens to prophets, Mackintosh never got much honour during his lifetime in his own land. And in the meantime, under pressure from the political regime in distant London, a great blight of English-style brick has been planted down in the country to house the working people. None the less, a country will not be denied. In the matter of piling stone upon stone, and brick upon brick, even in rearing in reinforced concrete and steel, native Scottish influences are again apparent in the housing schemes, schools and public buildings of Scotland.

The same influences that have kept Berwick not only a Scottish town but one that looks it after five hundred years of English dominion, have shaped and continue to mould the whole body of Scottish arts and the pattern of living.

Indeed, that is the whole point. A true nation is always marked off from its neighbours, not by the blood of the people, but by the country in which it lives. Though blown by the bag of a sheep, the pipes of Scotland with their stirring and, on occasion, haunting music could not have been evolved to their present perfection in any other land. The colours of the tartan are products of the alchemy of the seashore and the glens between the mountains. As the airs winged out of the Highlands the ballads were put to measure in the Lowland straths. The houses were hewn out of the native rock to match the clime of the country. Like the faith and the philosophy, the science and the industry, the whole way of living, dancing and singing came up from below. What was borrowed from other countries was always adjusted to suit the land.

CHAPTER ELEVEN

THE SCOT ABROAD

A CERTAIN wandering Monteith of obscure Scottish origin gained access, so the story goes, to the great Cardinal Richelieu in Paris. Asked from which side of the family he came, he remembered that his father cast his salmon nets in the Forth and promptly answered 'Monteith de Salmonnet'. Taken for one of the noblesse and as such introduced to fortune, he went on to found a line of De Salmonnets which became as proud of its titling as any real French de this or that, or German von the next thing.

The name of Robert Monteith de Salmonnet came, in fact, to be subscribed to a fat volume in French which dealt with 'The History of the Troubles of Great Britain. . . .' and which pitched into the English Earl of Clarendon for omitting 'the most remarkable passages in Scotland' during the wars of Montrose from his own account of the same troubles. Of course, things did not always go so well as that. On presenting himself as the Chef de Clan MacUisgebeatha (Mac Whisky), a great Highland chief was sent round to the cookhouse. And the Master (*Maître*) of Drummutchkin was told that the great man whose audience he sought was in no present need of a lawyer, Still and all, they took it better than that Archbishop of York who, on signing 'Ebor' to a bank cheque in Scotland, found himself in grave danger of being run in as a forger.

But right enough, on the whole, the great difficulty in franking titles and assessing social status in distant parts was, and remains, of no small advantage to the foreign faring Scot. James Boswell had that in mind in Germany when he did not stop to explain that when his father Lord Auchinleck retired, it was with Mrs. Boswell. When a student in the same country, the present writer found himself elevated to little less than a *Ritter*, and thus forgiven his national eccentricities, when his letters from home came addressed to him as Esq. After all, as his house fellows found out for themselves, and would take no denial, the dictionary meaning of 'Esquire' is 'attendant on a knight'.

To be quite serious, the Scot faring over the border and beyond the seas has always carried, and still does to-day, general credentials in his wallet that are denied to his English neighbour. In the old days it mattered quite a lot in socially conscious countries like England, France and Germany that he came from a land where territorial designations were scattered profusely over an otherwise barren waste. Since these could be picked up and appropriated by almost anyone, in the same way as Murray of Broughton styled himself after a paddock by the roadside, without benefit of any Lyon King of Arms, they did not mean very much in Scotland. Indeed to this day the farmers who till the soil with scant thought to armorial bearings are mostly all known after their holdings, as 'Laigh (low) Westermains'.

Nor indeed does this stop at farmers. Especially if he comes from an odd part, a very ordinary person may still be called 'Dingwall' or 'Dalbeattie', after the village or town of his origin. In his day, Robert Burns, as often as not, was known as Lochlea, Mossgiel or Ellisland, from the farms which he successively occupied. In the same way as the honorific Rectors of Scottish Universities to-day are sometimes invited to convene with ranking heads of seats of learning abroad, in the belief that they are, from their styling, active academicians, the wandering Scot was generally taken to be a landed, if somewhat impoverished gentleman, when that sort of thing counted. And of course, with his schooling he was just as generally able to carry it off.

Nowadays that advantage is now perhaps a little timeworn. But to make up for it, and be he ever so rascally in himself, he is never taken to represent a threatening power. He thus skips clear of that anti-great nation feeling which commonly troubles travelling Englishmen, North Americans, Germans and Russians. The 'English' or even the 'British' Prime Minister can thunder, bluster or falter as he will. But the wandering Scot, being classed with the Swiss, the Icelanders, the Monagasques or the Andorrans, dodges the trouble which is stirred up. It is by no means so trite as some may think that while the Englishman is dubbed a 'Limey' in the United States, a 'Pommie' in Australia and an 'Emmie' in New

Zealand, and usually with a sanguinary addition, the Scot manages along quite peacefully under the name of 'Scotty', 'Mac' or 'Jock'.

Moreover, straddling the distant times and the present, the wandering Scot, apart altogether from his education and personal parts, carries with him still another powerful recommendation. He rarely miscalls the country of his birth or origin, and by the same token, stands well with the land of his tarrying or adoption. That follows because the Scot has never been driven out of his own land in great numbers by starving hunger, like the Irish, by religious persecution, like the Huguenots, or by main force, like the Poles before the Germans or the Germans before the Poles. Hunger, persecution and force have moved small bodies. But in the main the Scot has gone freely abroad to seek his fortune and betimes to win fame in the finding of it.

Actually, Scots abroad are and always have been so laudatory about their native land, with a fidgety anxiety to keep its distinctions continually in open view, that people around them often wonder why they ever left it. The short answer to that is that the Scots always were a wandering people. According to the Declaration of Arbroath of 1320, they came from Scythia the Greater, through the Tuscan Sea, by the Pillars of Hercules and tarried a while in Spain before they reached Alba. Unlike the far trekking Vandals who were finally softened and dissolved amid the pleasures of Carthage, the Scots finally landed in a country by the edge of the ocean which hardened their bodies as it filled their minds. Making this land their home and calling it their own they were not long in sending parties back the other way.

To move into less fabulous times, the Scots were great travellers when the name of Scotia was still applied indiscriminately to Ulster and to present day Scotland. From these two bases, they first made their way back to the continent of Europe as missionaries, preaching the gospel. Some of their early Christianising, though not Romanising, settlements, like that at Ratisbon, are commonly attributed to the Irish. Not that it matters, but the confusion persisted until quite recent centuries. One has seen pictures of what were obviously Scots troops during the Thirty Years War subscribed in German books as *Irländer* or Irish.

More recently, there has been still more confusion. The Presbyterian Scots-Irish from Ulster, who played such a notable part

in founding and girding the United States, are often linked with
the Irish-Scots who live in Scotland today, a quite different race
of people.

After the missionaries came the scholars. Typified down
through the years by men like John Duns Scotus (the same whose
name is applied by inversion to the dunce in the corner), John
Mair or Major, Hector Boece and George Buchanan, these Scots
made their deep mark on European scholarships as they at the
same time brought back Continental learning to their native land.

That indeed was one of the many compensations for having
the Border closed and the Schools of Oxford shut against the
Scots during the long years of the Wars of Independence. Hand-
ling the language of Virgil as a living tongue, the Scots became
infinitely better Latinists than the more hermit English. As well
as that, they achieved a better mastery of the vernacular tongues
and of the general learning of Europe. John Knox, who, like his
reforming colleagues, dominated Latin, did a good deal of his
arguing with Mary, Queen of Scots in the French tongue. And,
of course, it took such as Sir Thomas Urquhart of Cromarty to
put curiosities and flowers into the English language by being
able to dispute, either in verse or prose, in any one of twelve
tongues, so he claimed for the Admirable Crichton.

The one thing common to all these wandering scholars and
indefatigable writers is that they all, each and every one of them,
sang the praises of their native land. Roman Catholic, Presbyterian, Episcopalian or plain philosophical, they all shouted the
name of Scotland aloud. That may have been a bit wearing on
their hearers and readers, but at least it denoted that to their mind
Scotland had something about it.

In the meantime, the soldiers and fighters had been taking their
way to Europe in increasing numbers. The movement set in and
gathered strength just after the Border was finally secured by the
battle of Bannockburn. During the Hundred Years' War between
France and England, the Scots took part in almost every battle.
Since their aim was the protection of their own land they fought
with a will.

Sometimes they slaughtered the English, as at Baugé in Anjou
in 1424. Sometimes they went down in the general defeat as at
the battle by Verneuil the following year. It was from the remnant
of Scots who survived that fight that Charles the Seventh of

France formed the famous *Garde Ecossaise*. That Guard was at first a prize-holding formation, with every one of its hundred men-at-arms and two hundred archers classed as a private gentleman. Though remaining a *corps d'élite*, it gradually became French in all but name. But as recently as 1730, the muster reply was, so they say, 'ai am hire' (I am here). A contingent of this Scots Guard which had been lent to Charles Stewart to further his Restoration in Britain hived off the Royal Scots Regiment, the First of the Line in the British Army.

Long before that, the Scots had been fighting in strength on other foreign battlefields. The armoured knights, like John, Earl of Buchan, who became Constable of France, and Archibald, Earl of Douglas, who rose to be Duke of Touraine, had fought with their retainers in terms of the Auld Alliance for the freedom and glory of Scotland. When the gun, the pike and the exploding mine became the arbiters of battle in the Thirty Years' War in the seventeenth century which made Germany an empty stinking shell of a country, these feudal formations gave way to captains and colonels, and to companies, battalions and brigades of enlisted men. The type of commander came to be portrayed by that formidable Dugald Dalgetty who clanks through Walter Scott's *Legend of Montrose*.

This time the Scots, who flocked overwhelmingly to the Protestant side, again enjoyed the respectability of fighting in their own cause. To that extent they ranked higher than absolute mercenaries. They were high above the Italian *condottieri* who killed anybody without question. However, they were no longer fighting for their country but for a party, religion and regular pay. Their bloodletting thus necessarily partook of the sordid characteristics of civil strife. Mostly on the winning side, they were never totally defeated. As Sir Thomas Urquhart gaily remarked, since there were always a few stray Scots with the other army, as they lost on one side they gained on the other.

Their greatest deeds were done under the banner of Gustavus Adolphus, the conquering King of Sweden. Yet, for all the limits of the cause, this training in arms in a very hard field with real powder and shot had a great deal to do with the preservation of the freedom of Scotland at home. The Scottish army which banded with Cromwell's Roundheads to rout the Cavaliers at Marston Moor during the War of the Commonwealth was officered and stiffened by men hardened in the German wars.

When the wars in Germany ended by exhaustion, many thousands of uprooted Scots were left to spread far and wide as traders and merchants. Being used to a hard country and a hard life, they roamed as pedlars all along the Baltic coast, and deep into Poland and Russia.

As their blood became diluted and their names vanished into the Slavonic mass (Lermontov the Russian poet was of Scottish descent) their solid good works remained. The churches, schools, hospitals and other foundations which they raised with their money may still be seen to-day in Holy Cracow and far into Muscovy. Like Patrick Gordon and Samuel Greig in Russia, and James Keith in Prussia, they still continued to serve and gain honour in lands other than their own. But by this time it was as individuals without companies of their own nation at their backs.

By then, the overlapping times had again changed. Scotland had got over the worst of her crippling poverty and the square-rigged ship was carrying settlers to distant lands far over the ocean.

When the Scots with their brethern from Ulster gained free entry into the American colonies, they threaded through the settlements of the English and other races on the coast. As fighting frontiersmen they plunged deep into the wilderness. In the fifty years after their arrival in numbers, following the rising of the Jacobites in 1715, the peopled area was trebled. With an axe in one hand, a rifle in the other and a Bible in their pouch (they were almost all Presbyterians) they turned their backs on the security of the Atlantic seaboard and pushed far to the west and south. Though they enjoyed no monopoly of colonial patriotism, it was the Scots beyond all others who prepared the way for the free United States. Not that they were all like minded on that issue, for they were numerous among the Loyalists who found their way to Canada.

Over the years they contributed a lot more than 'golf, thrift, jokes, square dances, trail ditties, whisky and Andrew Carnegie'. Though admittedly himself of Scottish extraction, John H. Finley of the *New York Times* claimed not so long ago: 'But for the Scots settlers, the independence of the colonies would not have been won, even if it had been declared. The Constitution would not have been such as to hold the States in a more perfect union.

The civilisation developed under it would not have had the moral
rigor and vigour, the adventurous individualism and the political
wisdom which have given it its distinctive character . . .'

For a start, it was Glasgow born Robert Dinwiddie (his name
is on the matriculation roll at the University) who, as Governor
of Virginia, broke the tight ring of the encircling French by dis-
lodging them from that Fort Duquesne which is now Pittsburgh.

At a time when the substantial men on the coast could see no
farther than their noses he raised troops and sent them a thousand
miles into the forest against the French on the great rivers. And,
most remarkably, he picked out young George Washington to go
with them, thus putting him in the way of that baptism of fire
and military training that set him out for preferment in command during the later Revolutionary War. The campaign cost
money. It was the reluctance to pay this, when all was won, that
led directly to the revolt, much more than that levying of British
duties on tea which brought about the Boston tea-party. Certainly Governor Dinwiddie did not consciously set all this in train.
He merely acted after the pattern of thought and action of his
nation.

More consciously, the generality of the Scots took the lead
among the colonists in founding churches and setting up schools.
Both the Presbyterian and Episcopalian churches which are now
so powerful in the United States stem from Scotland. So also does
the public system of education. The English contributed their
book of law, but it was mainly the Scots who drew up the Declaration of Independence on the formative model of their old
National Covenant. The document was written in the hand of
Charles Thomson, an Ulster Scot. Though numbering only about
seven per cent of the colonial population, nine among the fifty-
seven who signed it were of Scottish blood or birth. The Scots
then went on to provide the hard fighting core of Washington's
army. And when the fighting was over they played a leading part
in the Convention which came together to write the Constitution
of the new United States. Not surprisingly, from their proliferation of well educated ministers and dominies who burnished the
lamp of learning, the small Scottish minority provided twelve of
the fifty-four delegates. With the Rev. Dr. John Witherspoon,
who headed a group from Princeton University and who signed
the Declaration of Independence and taught James Madison,

said to be the main framer of the Constitution, James Wilson from St. Andrews towered among the gathering.

One cannot list all the names and contributions that followed. It must suffice to say that from that day to this, born Scots or men and women of Scottish blood have played a very notable part, out of all proportion to their numbers, in all fields of North American life. They have filled the ranks of the presidents (Wilson), judges (Marshall), statesmen (Hamilton), soldiers (MacArthur), sailors (Paul Jones), artists (Whistler), writers (Irving), scientists (Henry), scouts (Bowie), inventors (Bell), newspapermen (Bennett) and industrialists (Carnegie). The one thing that is hard to find in the United States is a Scottish name among the Tammany Hall politicians or the gangsters.

In any case, the present intent is not to detail the passage of history. It is to discover some thesis from the demonstrated fact that there have always been plenty of Scots willing to shout, like Patrick Henry before the First Continental Congress in Philadelphia on the 17th of October, 1774 : 'Give me liberty or give me death !' and to follow up with action; and they have always put sound arguments beside their weapons.

That the old grey country above the Cheviots does produce its own race of people is supported alike from the history of Canada, Australia, New Zealand, South Africa where English is spoken, and that of many other lands, like India, the Argentine and China where it is an acquired tongue.

It was kilted Highlanders, recruited after the 1745 Rising, who not only finally threw the French out of what came to be Pittsburgh, deep in the United States, but also scaled the Heights of Abraham to take their stronghold of Quebec and put Canada under the British Crown. The very heights were named after an old Scottish river pilot, Abraham Martin. As is not so well known, General Wolfe, who died in the battle, requited them very ill on that occasion.

'Put the Highlanders in the van,' he said. 'They are brave and intrepid, and it matters little if they fall.' They were more than brave and intrepid. As one party came after another, they adventured right across the plains and over the Rocky Mountains to the Pacific coast. There a young man from Stornoway in Lewis planted a blazed sign : 'Alexander MacKenzie from Canada by land, the 22nd of July, 1793 ... Lat. 52 degrees, 20 minutes,

48 seconds N.' It was that that set the northern boundary of the United States so far in the west, when the rule of that new country was still far east of the Rockies. It was of course two Scots who had most to do with the making of modern Canada.

These were William Lyon MacKenzie and John MacDonald. The first led the revolt of 1837 against the all too paternal British rule. The second drew up the British North America Act of 1867 under which the Dominion of Canada thrives to-day. It may as well be said that MacDonald, a Glasgow man, would readily have called it the Kingdom of Canada. But he was persuaded otherwise by the more timid British statesmen who did not want to offend the neighbouring republican United States.

It was much the same in Australia and New Zealand. There the mountains and rivers and the small towns, as well as some of the big ones like Perth and Brisbane in Australia, and Dunedin and Invercargill in new Zealand, all bespeak the Scottish pioneer. Leaving aside soldiering and politics, it was John MacArthur who put both these countries in the position to ride to wealth on the back of the sheep.

Coming from a sheep rearing country, he knew that the British breeds would be too coarse for the new dry lands under his eyes. He thus imported the Spanish merinos that are the main basis of the great flocks in those countries to-day. Now in these days only the wool could be shipped back to Europe. The rest of the sheep, like the fleshy body of the cattle, went to waste. It was still another Scot, John Harrison, a journalist, who introduced ship-borne refrigeration and put an end to that.

In Africa, the Scots, from Mungo Park to David Livingstone, were mostly associated with exploring. But in the persons of such as Leander Starr Jameson they had a great deal to do with the building up of South Africa and the Rhodesias and with the bringing up of the black colonies.

In India, they were mostly soldiers, traders, teachers and scientists. Nor when they became 'nabobs', did they forget their origin and kin. James MacRae, son of the Widow MacRae, a very decent washerwoman in Ayr, went to sea and was gone for forty years. When he at length returned he sought out his cousin Belle Gardner, wife of Hugh MacGuire, an itinerant fiddler. She had sheltered his old mother in her later years. Now rich from his long Governorship of Madras, he found husbands for all her four daughters and tochered (dowried) them well with lands and money. Leezie became wife to William, the thirteenth Earl of Glencairn. The second married an advocate who became Lord Alva. The third was paired off with MacRae's own nephew and set up on an estate at Houston. The fourth, the mistress of Orangefield, made her husband, Charles Dalrymple, a laird.

Not content with that, Governor MacRae presented the City of Glasgow with a metallic contrivance which over the years has sent countless drouths in the town to sign the pledge. That is the bronze equestrian statue of King William of Orange which, after years at Glasgow Cross, now stands near the Cathedral. In a fair wind, the metal horse wags its tail. Not knowing that that appendage has a ball and socket joint, well whiskied merry makers have been known, at the sight of it wagging, to sober up and make their way to the penitent stool. Which goes to show that a little misunderstanding, as in the case of Cardinal Richelieu with Monteith of Salmonett, can be no bad thing. To be sure, it has always been a good thing that Scots abroad are not easily classed as other than just plain Scots, with everyone a laird.

CHAPTER TWELVE

THE POLITICS OF SCOTLAND

A MAN, as the Gaels say in their wisdom, may himself draw a living out of the ground, but he cannot pull a fortune out of the sky unaided. To do by-ordinary well, he has to depend on some stroke of luck. It may be the picking up of a gold nugget or a lump of ambergris; it may be a fortunate or unfortunate concatenation of circumstances. For all his fearless heart and incisive, though simple, intellect, Field Marshal Viscount Montgomery would never have been in the position that he occupies to-day save that, in the general circumstances of war, General 'Straffer' Gott was shot down and killed.

Over the hundred years following the Union of the Parliaments in 1707, Scotland was attended by a powerful run of natural good fortune emanating, as we have already said, mainly from that very fruitful valley between the Clyde and the Forth. History is full of examples of one time strong nations that lost their freedom, not by any surcease of valour, or ebbing of skill, but by the lack of material means in new times. The Poles were a mighty nation fit to keep their borders against the Russians, Prussians and Austrians when bravery and levelled lances counted. They were torn apart when cannon and machinery, and the makings of these things, came to decide. The story of Ireland would have been entirely different if, by natural chance, coal and iron ore had been found under the bogs. Without these dead minerals, England would never have come to be the densely peopled and powerful country that it is to-day. Yet no man put these things in place.

By the year 1807, when Napoleon Bonaparte, who rampaged at will over the mainland of Europe, was raging at his inability to set foot on these islands, it seemed as if the worst fears of the evils which might come from the Parliamentary union with

England had been belied. With its middle belt by then a veritable power house, Scotland was well able to afford the treasure that flowed south to sustain the distant London government, as Peter's Pence drained over the Alps to Rome. The average cash income in Scotland came to be higher than that in England and remained so until the twentieth century.

The metal making and metal using trades which followed James Beaumont Neilson's invention of the hot blast added to the commercial and industrial strength of Scotland. But they also seeded many of the social and political problems that are sores to-day. Growing all too rapidly, they drained the Highlands and landward parts of human stock. And, since many Scots continued to venture abroad, they drew large bodies of common labour from Ireland. The Protestant Ulster-Scots, being taken for fellow countrymen, as they still are to-day, merged very speedily. But most of the incomers, with their descendants, being separated in social ideas and religion, have remained apart, by their own volition. That is not to say that there has not been a certain amount of mixing on the margins. But, broadly speaking, the Irish Roman Catholics have remained a race apart to the third and fourth generation and as such have become a political factor.

To assess the past course of events, to weigh up the problems that confront Scotland to-day, and to reckon the probabilities in the future, it is essential to grasp all this. One must also lay hold of the fact that, out of the natural gifts of the country, the laws and social ideas of Scotland were, and remain, quite different from those of England. The Scots never developed that mystique of social position which, as may be heard on the wireless and television any day, is the constant daily concern of the English. Wealth and political power were never drawn together in the same hands quite so tightly. Nor at other times were they set so much in opposition as they have been in England. The lord of the manor and the bishop, the squire and the vicar just do not fit into the Scottish scene. Neither do those hayseed yokels and aitch-dropping charladies that shuffle through the pages of *Punch*.

To be sure that worthy but very English journal portrays a world that is quite foreign to the average Scot. As such, it is sometimes excruciatingly funny in a way never intended by its learned and talented staff. Just as Walter Scott could not have written his stories south of Scotland, Charles Dickens could not have made the most of his, save in England. Both Mr. Bumble and Oliver Twist were typical English characters.

To take a particular point, the poor in England were set apart and pauperised over the centuries by being cast on compulsory parochial relief. As English historical economists, like Thorold Rogers, never tired of making as clear as can be, the poor laws of their country fostered habitual poverty.

In Scotland, on the other hand, the long custom was to relieve indigence by voluntary charity, mostly given at the church doors. There were plenty of beggars. But the simple and no doubt primitive system ensured that there was no permanently broken and pauperised class. Not being anything like so closely tied to the ground and dispirited, able bodied men could go to serve in arms abroad, as they did in great numbers. Like the far wandering pedlars, they hoped, if they survived, to come back with a competence. All this was possible in what came to be very nearly a theocratic, but strictly non-hierarchical state. Though Scots law had permitted rate-aided relief since 1569, the rapidly growing city of Glasgow did not resort to it until 1770, and then only in a small way. By 1800, fewer than a hundred parishes in Scotland levied a poor rate, and still only as an emergency measure.

As will presently be seen, this long continued very different treatment of the poor had a great deal to do with the trend in politics in Scotland more than a century later. The quite distinct Scottish attitude to crime had also a discernible effect on the widening of Scottish politics.

From the natural balance of the country, the central state machinery in Scotland was never very strong. The administration of criminal justice, as of most other affairs, had thus come to be very local. Some of the jurisdictions became hereditary and the remnant of these was not finally abolished until 1748. Seizing on this, some writers have made out that the barons and baillies could deliver anyone they liked to a dungeon or the hangman.

Doubtless, human nature and fallibility being what they are, there were a few miscarriages of justice. But the fact remains that the penal code of both the hereditary courts and of statute law, though harsh by present day standards, was infinitely milder than that of England. Public floggings, especially of women, were never a show in Scotland. Capital punishment which was freely dealt out in England for upwards of two hundred offences, some of them very trivial, was a comparative rarity in Scotland. There was never anything like the wholesale hanging of a dozen or so at a time that was a common spectacle at Tyburn in London, and all over England. In the twenty years before 1800 the number of executions in Scotland did not exceed six a year. This meant that the shootings and killings that were visited on the Scottish workers when they sought to combine towards the end of the eighteenth century created more of a stir and roused up more opposition than the same sort of arbitrary repression in England.

Another Scottish peculiarity that has had bearing on politics within the country in more recent times was the local rating system. (This has now been adjusted to the English pattern, but not before it spawned off a great deal of trouble which will take years to eradicate.) In the United States, the owner of a property pays all the local taxes. In England, the local rates fall on the occupier. In Scotland, however, the local rates were divided between the owner and the tenant.

As may be seen in any North American city, vacant houses that are eating their heads off stand little chance of survival. The same went in Scotland, though perhaps a little less urgently, since a vacant house paid only approximately half the local rates. It became the practice to take the roofs off houses that looked like lacking a paying tenant for any length of time. Hence the scarcity in Scotland of these old cottages, dower houses and ancient mills that are dotted all over England and are now, with a little renovation, very desirable residences. This de-roofing which sometimes had queer manifestations (one town council took the roofs off its own derelict property to save paying rates to itself) did not, however, affect the general provision of house room.

When rents were free to move, up to the Kaiser War, there was no shortage of dwelling houses in Scotland. In 1914 there were about 19,000 empty houses in Glasgow, so many that landlords were giving away keys with 'pounds of tea'. This plentitude of good, well maintained house room derived, in considerable part, from the way well doing working people invested their savings in stone and lime, especially in the smaller towns. They liked the feeling of acting the landlord and of pottering around their own small tenement properties. The virtual ban on housebuilding and the rise in construction costs during the war completely changed the scene. The Clydeside tenement dwellers took the lead in the agitation that led to the passing of the series of Rent Restriction Acts.

In the context of the Scottish rating system, and of the new burdens that were loaded on the local authorities (the relief of long continued worklessness had by this time been made a local charge) these Acts delivered Scottish housing to a vicious circle. As rates went up, the private landlords, who paid about half of them from their rents, were left with less and less money to cover their investment and to maintain the fabric of their buildings. The result was that private investment in working class houses for rent practically disappeared. At the same time increasing numbers of privately owned tenements which did not bring in enough to keep them in repair were left to the ravages of time, the wind and rain. The burden of providing artisan house room was thus thrown more and more on the local authorities.

In England, where the private landlord continued to get at least the same, and not less and less net rent, and where old tenant-less houses had been kept in being, the housing sore was far less acute. This crippling position, which became all the sorer after the Hitler War, had a great deal to do with the alignment of forces in Scottish local and national politics. A class of people developed who had a vested interest in houses that came to be increasingly supported from the local rates. These folk very naturally tended to support the Labour Party, which stood by the arrangement. At the same time, new industries tended to steer clear of localities with a higher than average rating burden. As Thorold Rogers pointed out, that happened long ago in those parts of England that committed themselves deeply to rate-aided poor relief.

In a necessarily brief commentary one cannot trace out in detail the far reaching consequences in politics of these sorts of issue. The bare bones of some of them have been strung together to point the thesis that politics in Scotland have been compounded of factors which in many cases differ profoundly from those in England, and sometimes do not even exist in that country. That in turn has affected the open attitude of the Scottish people to the vexed question of Home Rule.

Returning again to what may be called modern politics, there was hardly any such thing in Scotland a hundred years after the Union of the Parliaments. The sixteen Scottish peers who sat in the House of Lords balloted themselves and the forty-five members of the House of Commons were entirely unrepresentative.

The country was 'managed' from London, almost like a Colonial territory. Not that that seemed to matter much. The Kirk (though troubled by the imposition of patronage over its own head in 1711), Scots law, the schools, the organs of local government, and the broad way of life were all intact. Moreover the country as a whole was developing very vigorously in the enjoyment of very special advantages. It could well afford the financial drain of the connection with England. None the less, from the rapidity of change and the displacement of one trade by another, there were social stresses. For example, the weavers came into good times when spinning machinery was invented, but fell on evil days when weaving could be done on the power loom.

The Scottish workers were stirred by events in France. They formed combinations, rioted and were clubbed, and sometimes killed, just like their fellows in England. They were in no position to make a direct appeal to the Westminster Parliament. Nor, having no votes, could they press upon it indirectly. But they did push their case on occasion through the Scottish courts right up to the Court of Session. The Reform Act of 1832 passed a certain amount of political power to the middle classes. With the reorganisation of the constituencies, this could be exerted through Parliament. And it could impinge on the elected local councils which were set up. The still voteless generality continued to agitate for more security and better conditions, but for a long time without any marked resort to 'politics'.

The trade unions which had been formed frowned on the Chartism which swept England. Though that movement came to conferences and demonstrations in Scotland, it never actually reached fisticuffs. With their Kirk discipline and superior education, the Scottish workers preferred to rely on sober discussions and on mutual improvement. At a time when the English labourers were still sunk in illiteracy, improving classes and journals became all the go in Scotland.

The first move in the direction of practical working class politics came with the setting up of the Glasgow Trades Council in 1857. For a start it was called the Delegates of Trade.

In those days ordinary working people were unprotected against accident, illness and the loss of their jobs. The Scottish able bodied poor, as will be remembered, could not be cast upon the local rates in any degree. The new Trades Council, which from the first combined a number of crafts, advised the Town Council that its object was 'to endeavour to obtain work, or in the absence of that, to use every legal means to provide food, clothing and shelter for the unemployed . . .'. In the true spirit of the Scottish missionary, the Glasgow body did the spade work in setting up a similar organisation in London in 1860. Announcing that it was aware that 'many are opposed to trades meetings being mixed with politics', it then ventured into that field. The first main aim was to extend the Parliamentary franchise.

To that end, the Glasgow men went on to convene in London the first all-British conference of trade unionists. The affairs of that conference came under the notice of the House of Commons. That led in turn to the founding of what was then called the National Trades Union Congress in 1868. When that Congress dismissed local Trades Councils from its representation in 1895, the Glasgow Trades Council again took the lead in forming, in 1897, what is now the Scottish Trades Union Congress. That differs from the (British) Trades Union Congress in having no block vote and in giving representation to local Trades Councils, apart from Unions. One may claim, therefore, that the organised and linked trade union movement in Britain is very largely of Scottish origin, and a product of the Kirk and the Scottish schools.

The extension of the franchise by the next Reform Act put the commonalty more directly into politics. Significantly, one of the first fruits of this was the embodiment of the Scottish Home Rule Association in 1886. That was a year after a Secretary for Scotland had been reappointed after a lapse of 140 years. Unfortunately the Association, like the Highland Land League, was bedevilled by events in neighbouring Ireland. Home Rule for that unhappy country was associated with 'Rome Rule' and Land Leaguism with blunderbusses. Until then, the pressure for reform had been channelled through the Liberal Party, which ruled the roost in Scotland. Indeed the Conservative Party did not come to any power in Scotland, until it was set in opposition to the new Labour Party.

However, both these Scottish bodies struck out for themselves when they stood behind James Keir Hardie in Mid-Lanark in 1888 as the first ever 'Labour' candidate. The honorary secretary of the London Committee of the Scottish Home Rule Association was none other than that James Ramsay MacDonald who ultimately forgot his youthful allegiance and became British Prime Minister. His letter of encouragement linked 'the cause of Labour and of Scottish Nationality'. James Keir Hardie made self-government for Scotland the main plank on his platform. He cried : 'Until we have a Parliament of our own, we cannot obtain the many and great reforms on which the people of Scotland have set their hearts . . .'. That was reasonable enough since, with the new breadth of the voting public, Parliamentary representation from Scotland had come to be far more radical than anything likely to come to the front in England.

Hardie was defeated at the polls. (He was returned later for West Ham in London largely due to the notice he had won from his activities in Scotland.) But he called his supporters together and formed the Scottish Labour Party. In addition to advocating 'the state acquisition of railways' and 'the issue of State Money only' that pioneer party also stood for Home Rule. However it lost its identity and its original purpose out of its own missionary efforts. Taking up a motion that had been passed at a meeting of the British Trades Union Congress in Glasgow (and passed three times previously in England, but neglected) it went on to organise a meeting in Bradford which ended with the foundation of the Independent Labour Party in 1893. The British Labour Representation Committee followed in 1900 and the Parliamentary Labour Party in 1906.

Like the Trades Union Congress, the Labour Party which exists and carries on to-day, perhaps in more senses than one, is a fruit of Scottish endeavour and in the ultimate of the Presbyterian Kirk. The Scots took the lead because they were on the whole much better lettered and because, apart altogether from the aspirations of the working masses, they wanted Home Rule for their country.

However, as the English crowded into the 'movement' the voice of Scotland became ever weaker. A succession of Scottish Home Rule bills were put before the Westminster Parliament. Some of them had a favourable first reading; but they never came to anything. The English Labour men were naturally more concerned with converting Liberals and Conservatives than with furthering the Scottish Home Rule ideas of James Keir Hardie.

Nor was it long before support for Scottish Home Rule became a thing of straw in the higher circles of the Labour Party and the now closely associated trade unions, even in Scotland. Partly it was a case of the new gospel of Socialism supervening over all else. But the land change between Scotland and London had a great deal to do with it. As the political candidates won seats and the trade union organisers rose higher in the hierarchy, they naturally fancied themselves as strutting more to purpose and concomitant fortune in the broader and lusher fields of England. In the Labour Party, support for Home Rule for Scotland died away to still small voices from the body of the hall. It was all very well to advocate Home Rule for every other place under the sun. The matter of paying more than lip service to Home Rule for the oldest nation in Europe was postponed until the 'Greek Kalends'.

In spite of the long association of the Labour Party with Scottish Home Rule and a lingering feeling that it might return to its original loyalties, a new alignment of Scottish political opinion might have taken place much earlier than it did but for those peculiarities of Scottish poor relief and local rating that have already been outlined.

One must bear in mind that until the Kaiser War Scotland was on the whole a prosperous country, as has been evidenced in other parts of this work. Vouching for this, steel output in Scotland in 1920 was no less than 23 per cent of the whole British total, that is to say more than double the population ratio. There were trade and industrial troubles, but nothing deep seated and truly chronic.

Though the very rudimentary system of poor relief which had nourished Scottish virtue in the past was now hopelessly out of date, it was just made to serve. However, with the very deep and long continued depression of the early twenties, many thousands of otherwise well doing people found themselves with no means of support. Having exhausted their covenanted benefit at the Labour Exchange, they could not go 'on the parish' as in England. Their only recourse was the poor-house legislation permitting rate-aided local relief, which was pushed through hurriedly. But though the new poor rate soared, the machinery creaked badly and the misery was both serious and widespread. It was out of the reaction against this misfortune that the Labour Party first won seats in numbers in Scotland. The Red Clydesiders who stormed Westminster did so by malefit of the then deficiencies of the Scottish poor law.

Later on, the same party has been sustained out of the defects in the Scottish rating system, in the new times of rent restriction. From the discomfiture of the private landlords, the Scottish local authorities were compelled to build housing schemes on a larger scale than in England. More so since, as a heritage from the economical past, notions of a fitting rent are much more modest in Scotland than in England, these drew more and more from the public purse. The average council house rent is no more than 8s. 8d. a week in Scotland as a whole, and a mere 2s. 10d. in Dunbartonshire. Taking the place of the former crippling load of local relief, which is now a charge on the national Exchequer, the new rate burden has discouraged industry, now all the more since factories have been rated on half their valuation.

The point is of course that people do not really probe very deeply into the origins of their troubles. With their jobs insecure and a vested interest in low rate aided rents, housing scheme tenants tend to be continuing stalwarts for the Labour Party. Manifestly, a native Scottish government, of whatever political colour, would be much closer to the problem and in a better position to deal with it before it degenerates to extremity. Full time professional politicians do not see it that way, however. After the first flush of crusading enthusiasm has gone, their interest, taking the average, is to keep their seats at all costs.

Home Rule for Scotland diffused into a mild sentiment in the decaying Liberal Party before it was squeezed out between the ranged forces of Capital and Labour.

The rising Labour Party proved to be a broken reed. Through growing out of the demand for self-government in Scotland it came to the point of lambasting even mild Home Rulers as 'Tartan Tories'. In the face of the great social arguments the whole question was obscured. Ultimately, in a land which is by nature radical and which was a citadel of Liberalism, the field was given over to the contending Labour and Conservative Parties.

Against that background, the Scottish National Party was formed in 1928. As a frankly political party, with one simple message, it succeeded in getting its banner bearer, Robert

MacIntyre, returned for Motherwell and Wishaw in 1945. In the meantime, Scottish Convention had hived off under John MacCormick in 1942 to pursue a more general and non-political line.

That body tested the deep down Scottish feeling by getting over two-and-a-half million adults of every class to sign the National Covenant. It also convened a succession of very broadly based and successful National Assemblies in Edinburgh. Some of its junior adherents stirred the national spirit when they made off with the Stone of Destiny from Westminster Abbey. It later merged into the Covenant Association.

Many other groups have pressed the claims of Scotland, like the Scottish National Congress, a small body which outwardly stands by passive resistance but which none the less is exceedingly active. It was largely inspired by Roland Muirhead, an old-timer who has taken part in the whole of the play since the time of the Scottish Home Rule Association and the early Scottish Labour Party. For the rest, various other smaller organisations like the Scottish Patriots under Wendy Wood and the Scottish Plebiscite Society are in the field.

It is true enough that up to the present the Scottish National Party, the only body with direct political aims at a national level, has not had any electoral success, save for the brief excursion of Robert MacIntyre. But the Home Rule groups have steadily increased their impact and have seated quite a number of members or supporters on local councils. With the help of the Scottish Liberal Party, which is pledged to Home Rule, they managed to get the Conservative Government to appoint a Royal Commission on Scottish Affairs in 1952. Though more concerned with discovering arguments against rather than in favour of Scottish self-government, that body recommended certain minor devolutionary changes.

Since then, the wheels have continued to grind slowly, in the general direction of more devolution. For the reason that the more centralised the policy, the more executive control has to be passed out to the regions, this trend is bound to gather force. Though still without any diagnosis of the real nature of the troubles presently afflicting Scotland, the Conservatives are now, for the first time, paying heed to Scottish, as Scottish, opinion. The Scottish section of the Labour Party, now denied preferment in London, is also tending to come back to its base in Scotland. There is once again a recognisable Scottish Labour point of view. But as there have been changes before, like the virtual disappearance of the once all powerful Liberal Party in Scotland, there may be changes again.

The two big parties that are now apparently so firmly settled may find the Scottish ground moving from under them. Now that the social question has been resolved by the advent of the more or less affluent society, the Conservatives, who are by nature Anglican, are constantly making barbs for themselves. For instance, for the mere sake of tidy administration, they cut bank credit in Scotland to match the quite different position in England. The Labour Party, for its part, is now coming to be more and more associated with poverty than with overflowing prosperity. On top of that, it has got mixed up with sectarian politics in the industrial areas. Indeed it has come to depend, especially in some districts, on the Roman Catholic vote. In its early days it was of course secular on one side, and evangelical on the other.

One big point is that Scotland can no longer afford the financial cost of too close an incorporation with England, as it well could do, in its stride, up to the First World War. Nor, being quite a different country, with different bases and ideas, can it afford to be delivered to policies which, however favourable to England, do not suit the old grey land. Out of that, if the past is any guide, the ball will sooner or later be put back into play right in Scotland, and among quite different groups of players. As the Scots say, the day will keek (peep) through a sma' hole. The future of politics in and for Scotland is not to be assessed on the outward appearances of to-day. Come late or early, the old country will intrude itself. No association of men can prevent that.

CHAPTER THIRTEEN

THE FREEDOM AND FORTUNE
OF SCOTLAND

'Ah! Freedom is a noble thing!
Freedom makes man to have liking!
Freedom all solace to man gives!
He lives at ease that freely lives!
A noble heart may have none ease,
Nor else nought that may him please,
If freedom fail.'

JOHN BARBOUR, the first great poet in the Scots tongue, and an historian to boot, voiced that thought (Englished for the common reader) in the latter half of the fourteenth century.

It sets out the general case for a Scottish Parliament, framed to Scottish needs and philosophy, and charged with full powers to govern the land, in free communion with neighbouring England. No more than a man, a nation cannot live freely at ease, and flourish, without essential liberty. That simple sentiment will be endorsed, and again underlined, by every true born Englishman, as well as by every leal (loyal) Scot.

If the foregoing discussion has served its purpose, it will be agreed that Scotland is the home, not only of a nation, but also of that nation which first set itself apart as such in all Europe. That came about by the interplay of a great many related racial, linguistic, historical, topographical, geographical, and geological factors.

Compounded out of unchanging elements, the final alchemy would have been much the same, regardless of the blood, tongue and customs of the original peoples who settled in the land. The seed of the Northumbrians who first brought the Saxon tongue to Scotland are as true Scots to-day as the Gaels of the mountains, the broken seaboard and the islands who to this day cleave to the language of ancient Alba. A great many regional differences, marked by varied customs, habits, tongues and modes of life, remain in Scotland. They will persist as long as the mountains stand, the wind blows and the tides run. But a very strong bond forged in the fires of circumstance unites the farmer with his broad Scots, the crofter-fisherman with his Gaelic, the industrial worker with his townie argot, and the professional man with his lettered English.

The resistant qualities of Scottishness have been carried over the Appallachians in North America, into the Arctic wastes of Canada, deep into empty Australia, over the grazing lands of New Zealand and into many other lands. In these countries the time will doubtless come when the passage, settling and mighty shaping work of the Scots will be forgotten by the generality. The mighty Goths are now one with the dust in Italy. Alexander's men have left little apparent in India save a slight fairing of the skin. But in Scotland the land will continue to bear and ripen the same fruits. It was the fortune of Scotland that the land was protected against overturning invasions and that stratification in society which goes with conquest and has been the lot of England. It was the continued good fortune of the country that the broken land itself prevented the theft of freedom from within.

As times advanced, and great threatening forces gathered on the Border, it was the continuing great good fortune of Scotland that the bowels of the earth provided the material means for independence. And all along, the old country, with nothing beyond it but the stormy ocean, has remained a difficult frontier land, repugnant to that softness of life which took the fibre out of the once sturdy Vandals when they drew up their wagons under the palms of Africa. To take a homely illustration from the market place, the snell (chilly) windswept fields of Scotland provide such seed potatoes for the rich fields of England as the English themselves can never contrive to rear. The same goes for the natural human stock of the country.

That the nationhood of the Scots was a strong thing may be seen from the fact that it was not one whit abated when, largely out of an historical chance, the Crowns of the Scottish people and of the realm of England (a very telling difference) were put under one head in 1603. That it continued strong is evidenced from the fact that two hundred years after the Estates of Scotland were merged with the Parliament of England in the confused times of 1707, the institutions of Scotland had come to be even more differentiated from those of neighbouring England. For all the 'management' from England, the Presbyterian Kirk, the corpus of Scots law, the schools and the philosophy of the country were even more national than in past times.

Certainly, there were interchanges, as between any two neighbours. Superficialities spread over the two lands, as they are now flowing over all the countries of the earth that seek to be civilised. But they had no more real effect on the heart and soul of the essential Scotland than, as one hopes, the importation of 'tin pan alley' confections has on the culture of England. As the Channel in time set the English apart from those peoples in Europe whose blood they share, the broad Border kept the Scots separate, and all the more so since it screened an entirely different sort of land. Nor indeed were the kingly and Parliamentary unions without their advantages. They opened the way for the free egress of people who found England more to their liking, and for the ingress of others who preferred the sharper air of Scotland.

Right enough, the Border, now no more a tight hermetical seal, has tended to function like one of those curious membranes that permit certain chemicals to pass in one direction, while others go in the exact opposite. For instance, all to the good of Scotland, the English 'public' schools attract types who, once they are conditioned to English ways, can no longer return to move freely in Scotland. That selective culling and removal of the progeny of what the Germans call the *wunderkinder*, those who having acquired wealth like nothing better than showing it, has had a great deal to do with the preservation of the Scottish way of life. In Scotland a man is still either known by his first name among his familiars or by his appropriate title of 'Mr.' among all others.

One does not say that socially classifying forces are not always at work in Scotland, as in all countries. But as they were denied by the broken land in the past, they are now relieved by the handy presence of England. More than in most countries, status in Scotland, so near England, still goes more by character, accomplishment and good manners, than by wealth and power.

One remembers the Highland boatman who sat impassively on his oars while a boatload of convivial English 'gentlemen' failed to catch a single fish. He explained : 'Puir English gentlemen

they were, naethin' aboot them except a pickle siller. If I couldna'
be drinkin' wi' them, as one man wi' anither, I couldna' be showin'
them hoo tae land a salmon.'

Since the main national institutions were unimpaired, indeed
were stronger than ever, and the country was thriving mightily
from the spate of new inventions that exactly suited it, no great
issue was made when English styled organs of local government
were introduced following the passage of the Municipal Reform
Act of 1833. The old Scottish bodies had served very well in their
day. By their very local embodiment, and from the balance of
interests which characterised Scotland, they were far from being
the autocratic conclaves that their self-perpetuation would suggest. However they seemed to fall short in an age when public
representation by way of the ballot of the generality had come
on the scene.

At that time it really hardly mattered over very large sections of Scottish life where the actual Government was housed.
On many counts, it might as well have been in Timbuktu. The
Scots were finding plenty of self expression both at home and
abroad. They mustered far more than their proportionate share
of the Fellows of the Royal Society in London. At the same time
the bulk of the ranking Scottish scientists found their native land
congenial. The most of them lived, worked and died in the
country. With pipers, and the drummers that had been put beside
them, Scottish regiments fought on every battlefield in the colours
and to the sounds of their country. Scotsmen of every class played
a very full part in building up the British Empire. Scottish industry and commerce was conducted by natives of the land and
their ramifications reached all over the world.

Complete with the kilt and that very independent John Brown
who kept Queen Victoria in her womanly place as her consort
Prince Albert never could (and indeed much to her inner satisfac-
tion), the Royal Family went in fulsomely for 'Balmorality'. The
old joke about the visiting Scot who saw no Englishmen in
London but only 'heids o' depairtments' warmed the simple Scottish heart. The matter of Home Rule was no more than a vague
sentiment.

It first began to harden into an aim when it was observed that,
as the hand of the London administration became steadily more
evident, Scotland hardly ever got the government it voted for.

For ninety years after the passage of the Reform Act of 1832, Scotland almost always voted strongly Liberal. Very often the Liberal majority in the House of Commons depended on the Celtic Fringe.

When the Conservatives were in office they were faced with a politically hostile Scotland. It was the feeling of being chained to, and kept back by an alien political philosophy that put power into the first considered moves for Home Rule. As James Ramsay MacDonald put it in a letter to James Keir Hardie, the Scottish Home Rule Association sought to 're-construct' Scottish Liberalism, by giving it more radical expression. In the face of the long succession of Parliamentary polls where the Scots ranged on one side and the English on the other, that logically calls for setting up a separate federal Parliament. Most English people will surely agree that they would not like to be bossed around by a political régime of quite the opposite complexion from that for which they continually vote.

If a palpably un-English régime were maintained in office at Westminster for a hundred years by votes piled up in Scotland, one fancies that the people of South Britain would eventually become very sore about it. In the end, if no other recourse offered, they would put the Scots right out of the general comity. The Scots were in that galling position for the best part of a century. By nature radical, and moved by quite different considerations from the Irish 'Home Rulers', they could not adopt the same obstructive and landlord-shooting tactics. For all that, a separation, leading to an amicable federation, might have come to pass long ere this but for the First World War. Just before that burst out, to alter everything in Europe, the Liberal Government declared that a Bill providing for Scottish Home Rule would follow the passage of an Act dealing with Ireland.

The Kaiser War changed the whole course of British politics. Within the general context, it also brought about an abrupt reversal of the economic condition of Scotland. For over a century the very thriving power using, metal working, capital goods producing and exporting industries had enabled Scotland to bear the cost of the English connection while still improving the standard of the generality. (As the North of England people are now well aware any highly centralised government like that presently crowded in London necessarily draws away much more from the periphery than it puts back.) These industries, which furnished the added margin of advantage, over and above the other trades, suddenly collapsed. At the same time they became subject to great labour-saving technological changes.

For the first time, Scotland was greatly troubled by a mass and long enduring unemployment problem. To make matters worse, the central government in London, which had greatly increased its scope of action during the war, kept on interfering more and more in every department of life. Scottish industry, having lost the natural impetus which had carried it ahead for so long, was knocked about and put off balance. Unfortunately, the sudden impact of these misfortunes split the social entity of the country. The Liberal Party, which had been dominant for generations and which was broadly National, faded away rapidly. The field was shortly given over almost wholly to the contending Conservative and Labour Parties. There were naturally many involved reasons for this.

Centuries earlier, the Presbyterian Kirk was helped and consolidated beyond all measure by the historical accident of the properties of the former Roman Catholic Church falling mainly into private hands. This built up a powerful vested interest against Episcopacy in quarters which would normally have been expected to support that church system. In the same way, the Labour Party drew a powerful advantage from the survival of the voluntary Scottish system of poor relief. It proved inadequate in the new, very hard times. Before new measures to take its place could be brought into tune, the 'Red Men' from the Clyde were already Members for Misery at Westminster. The position thus obtained was further strengthened when the new Rent Restriction Acts, allied to the Scottish rating system, brought about the decay of housing.

Much more than in England, the Scottish local councils were forced to build subsidised houses very extensively. As their vested interest in cheap, state- and rate-aided houseroom became more and more evident, the people in these houses tended to support the Labour cause. With no great attention being paid to the niceties of social doctrine the Labour paladins became Members for Housing. With the disappearance of the secular socialist gospel, working class Roman Catholics who had previously been as good as forbidden to vote for 'Godless Socialists' came to give the Labour

candidates great electoral support. (Many early recruits to the
Labour Party were put out of the Roman Catholic church.)

By natural action and reaction, all this in turn has lent a good
deal of solid support to the Conservatives. Associating them with
Ulster Unionism, working class Orangemen, who are numerous
in many industrial areas in Scotland, are preponderantly Conservative. Out of this, the much loved James Maxton by no
means got it all his own socialist way in artisan Bridgeton, in
Glasgow. Though nothing very much ever comes out in public,
Labour politics in many industrial parts of Scotland, as in Coat-
bridge, are now dominated by Roman Catholics. Contrariwise,
Conservative politics in places like Motherwell are very largely in
the hands of Orangemen. Depending on the weight of local voting
power, many Labour candidates get their ticket as representing
or going against the Roman Catholic interest. This situation,
common enough in Australia, is foreign and indeed out of this
world over most of England.

This odd and unnatural alignment in Scottish politics was
even more clearly defined by the Hitler War. Apart altogether
from the Labour Party's initial success (mainly, as it happened,
supported from England) and the drive for nationalisation, the
successive régimes tended to retain and even extend the central
controlling powers which had fallen to the government during
the conflict. All this boded ill for Scottish industry, more so since
it had been unable to make away with any noticeable share of the
new consumers' goods trades that had grown to stature over the
past generation. Whereas it did not matter a crack a hundred or
even fifty years ago that Scotland was four hundred miles away
from London, it came to matter more than somewhat that Scottish commercialists and industrialists were farther away than a
taxicab ride to Whitehall.

For some mysterious, or perhaps not so mysterious reason, the
Scottish coal industry which was near the head of the production
table, and near the foot of that setting out costs, in 1947 came,
in a few brief years, into a parlous condition of low output and
high costs. From that, as it would not have done a dozen years
ago, it has taken a good brunt of the cutback in coal raising. With
one thing added to another, it became evident that, whatever
might be the unemployment rate in England, that in Scotland was always at least twice as heavy, in good times and bad.

This timeously supplied another good rallying cry to the Labour Party. Its 'Members for Socialism' who became 'Members for Misery', then 'Members for Housing' now became 'Members for Work'. It is largely this that explains how the Labour Party which never swept the polls as it did in England after the war, has none the less maintained its position better in Scotland, up to the present.

Much more than any rivalry of 'Capitalism' and 'Socialism' these questions about poor relief, subsidised housing, and worklessness, with the veiled religious contention, have made up the warp and woof of Scottish politics these last forty years. The issue of a Scottish Parliament has thus tended to be overlooked.

The mind of the Scots to 'gang their ain gait' has been voiced freely enough in a series of test plebiscites and questionnaires. It came out very definitely in the mass signing of the National Covenant and in the rejoicing which attended the lifting of the Stone of Destiny. Many worthy people were, or professed to be, shocked at that ploy, but the great majority more than enjoyed the discomfiture of the Dean of Westminster. The poets, balladiers and songsters had a high old time turning out new lays and ditties to old tunes. But this feeling has been rarely reflected at the Parliamentary polls. None the less, there are clear signs that the cry of the Conservatives that a vote for Home Rule would be a vote for Socialism and the curiously similar warning of the Labour people against 'Tartan Tories' are wearing thin and reedy.

Both these monied interests are now indeed more and more inclined to go well out of their way to cater to, and placate Scottish opinion. The Conservatives are clear enough minded (as regards their ranking leaders) to see that if they hope, as they do, to maintain themselves in power semi-permanently, it will be a bad thing if the sore is kept running in Scotland. For their part, the Scottish Labourites, now that they are pushed out of prominence and hope of preferment at Westminster, are tending to return to their home base. Since the two big parties are almost equally divided in Scotland, with thirty-five seats apiece and only one in the grip of the Liberals, but that firmly in Orkney and Shetland, the position in Scotland offers hope and fear, to both.

The claims of Scotland as a whole, which, for many years, could scarcely be heard above the din about the false issues, are now more and more receiving attention from the two contending parties. Truly, when thieves fall out the honest man comes into his own. And he comes into his own all the quicker when the robbers, who are for the most part confidence men, lose their deftness of touch and ready tongue. The Conservatives for example, keep on rubbing the Scots the wrong way when they fail to see that Elizabeth the Second of England is still only Elizabeth the First of the Scots. More seriously, they damage their prospects in quarters likely to give them most support when they cut bank credit in Scotland to match a slash in England, in aid of no more than tidy administration.

The Labourites, on their side, rather spoil their case when they advocate Home Rule for every country under the sun, and loudly, and make an exception of Scotland. And they mute their Britishism when they call conferences to deal with Scottish affairs, as Scottish issues. The other day the Scottish Trades Union Congress accepted the Scottish case by default, even if it did not realise it, when it brought together in Glasgow all the members for constituencies in Scotland (not all of them Scots) for the first time in 253 years. In the meantime, the stock argument that conjoined countries cannot separate, and then federate, due to the intimate intertwining of their commercial interests is being denied every day. It is also becoming clear that, far from drawing financial support from England, great sums are drained out of Scotland to feed the great maw of London.

Right enough, the new fortune of Scotland lies in the probability that, as Edward, Earl of Clarendon, observed in his *History of the Rebellion and Civil Wars in England Begun in the Year* 1641, 'neither of those Parties have the game in their hands, as they have formerly perhaps fancied to themselves'. Still another bounty is that if the age of consumers' good production, taking in motor cars, radios and such like, did not suit Scotland and brought about comparative poverty (though not absolute), the new age of atomic power production certainly does. It happens that the wind and the water which carried and preserved Scottish song, and with it the old doric tongue, are exactly what the natural philosopher (physicist) needs to control and get the most out of the disintegrating atom.

It may be too that the English people, when they become more fully aware of the quite different expression of life and opinion in Scotland may conceive it in their own interest to have a friendly neighbour rather than a grumbling lodger. They have nothing to lose, but a lot to gain from a friendly Scotland, if only the pleasure of 'going foreign' without having to master a language other than their own. They may realise that that 'freedom which is a noble thing' which they themselves have preserved against assault from within and without, is just as highly prized a heritage of the Scots.

'A noble heart may have none ease, nor else nought that may him please, if Freedom fail. . . .'

It is the great and constantly abiding good fortune of Scotland, that it was the first land in all broad Europe to set itself apart as the home of a nation. There have always been Scots to cherish and fight for that freedom. Nature has been kind in providing the means to preserve it. The day will surely come, and perhaps sooner than later, when, as in 1603 and again in 1707, another calvalcade will take the road. This time it will be to the North to attend the opening of the new Estates of Scotland.

On that day Scotland will have found much else besides a company of legislators, meeting in the land that chose them. As they fall to talking (to profit, or to the lack of it, as makes no matter), it will have grasped its newly burnished birthright—that essential Freedom which 'all solace to man gives' even if the roof falls over his head. And the Kingdom of England, than which there is no other better in all the world, save that of the Scots, will have won quit of a surly lodger and found an understanding friend.

INDEX

Aberdeen, 40, 51, 52, 66, 87, 92, 100;
   University 43, 51
Abraham, Heights of, 113
Academies (Schools), 50, 55
Accountancy profession, 77
Advocates, Faculty of, 35
Aiden, Saint, 17
' Alba ', 17, 129
Albert, Prince Consort, 131
Alexander III, 24-25, 87
Alloway, 104
Anderson, Professor John, 56, 74
Angus, Archibald Douglas, Earl of, 23
Antonine's Rampart, 16
Arbroath, 43, 66;
   Declaration of, 20, 21, 25, 108
Ard Tong, 20
Argyllshire, 17
Army Act, 37
Atomic power, 82-83
Auchinleck, Lord, 65, 90, 106
' Auld Alliance ', see French Alliance
Auld Lichts, 47
Australia, 113, 114, 129
Ayrshire, 20

Baillies, 36
Baliol, John (King), 62
Balmoral Castle, 105, 131
Bank of England, 76
Bank of Scotland, 76
Bannockburn, Battle of, 25, 109
Baptists, 39
Barbour, John, 87, 128
Barr, Rev. James, 48
Barrie, Sir James Matthew, 98-99
Baugé, Battle of, 109
Beaton, Cardinal David, 29
Beatons, of Mull, 86
Becket, Thomas à, 29
Bell, Alexander Graham, 113
Bell, Joseph, 35
Bennett, James Gordon, 113
Berwick-on-Tweed, 10, 19, 105
Bessemer, Henry, 79

' Betty Burke ', 91
Black, Professor Joseph, 70, 71, 73, 74
Board of Manufacturers, 101
Boece, Hector, 109
Bonaparte, Napoleon, 91, 116
Book of Policy and Discipline, 42
Boswell, James, 35, 65, 90, 95, 106
—, Sir Alexander, 90
' Bothy Ballads ', 92
Boulton, Matthew, 75, 78
Bowie, James, 113
Braxfield, Lord, 36
Bridie, James, see Mavor, O. H.
Brindley, James, 54
British Linen Bank, 76
British North America Act, 1867, 114
Brown, John, 131
Bruce, King Robert, 25, 62, 87
—, Marjory, 27
Buchan, John, Earl of, 110
Buchanan, George, 51, 89, 109
Burghers, 47
Burns, Robert, 47, 56, 65, 85, 90, 92,
   93, 94, 97, 104, 107
Bute, Isle of, 78

Cade, Jack, 63
Caithness, 17
Caledonia, 16, 19
Calvin, John, 103
Cambuskenneth, 62
Canada, 13, 111, 113, 114, 129
Carham, Battle of, 18
Carnegie, Andrew, 111, 113
Ceilid'h, 98
Charles I, 46
Charles VII (of France), 109-110
Chaucer, Geoffrey, 87, 88
Church of England, 38, 39
Church of Scotland, 38-48, 52-53, 60,
   63, 64, 65, 80, 92, 97, 102, 109, 112,
   121, 123, 130, 133;
   General Assembly, 42, 44, 46, 47, 51
Christianity, Early, 16, 17
Clarendon, Edward, Earl of, 106, 136